Island Home

Why People Come to Martha's Vineyard and Why They Stay

Elaine Pace

The profits from the sale of this book will be shared with the Island Food Pantry of Martha's Vineyard

Island Home

Why People Come to Martha's Vineyard and Why They Stay

Elaine Pace

© Elaine Pace 2008

www.memories101.us

Cover photograph: Gay Head Light at the clay cliffs in Aquinnah

Published by 1stWorld Publishing
1100 North 4th St. Suite 131, Fairfield, Iowa 52556
tel: 641-209-5000 • fax: 641-209-3001
web: www.1stworldpublishing.com
Book design: Liz Howard: liz@1stworldpublishing.com

First Edition

LCCN: 2008924399
Hardcover ISBN: 978-1-4218-9852-0
Softcover ISBN: 978-1-4218-9853-7
eBook ISBN: 978-1-4218-9854-4

A Heartfelt Journey of Discovery and Self-fulfillment

"The author has found a unique way to portray Martha's Vineyard. By interviewing an eclectic group of "newcomers," she tells how they came here, why they stayed, and what they have given back to the island. Her conversations show the reader what makes the Vineyard so different from the rest of the world."
   —**Edo Potter,** "Wash-ashore"
   Chappaquiddick Resident of 74 Years

"Elaine Pace made her own transition to the Vineyard some years ago, and now she lovingly extracts from other islanders who've done the same. Their journeys—physical, personal, and spiritual—help to shed light on our own erstwhile paths."
   —**Holly Nadler,** Author

"Island Home captures the essence of many "wash-ashores" —a very personal portrayal..."
   —**Dave Stein,** CEO: ES Research Group

"Elaine Pace is honest and insightful—*Island Home* is a delightful read..."
   —**Judith A. Fisher,** MD, Martha's Vineyard Hospital

"A warm and telling portrait of a vital but often-overlooked part of the Vineyard community..."
   —**Dan Waters,** Poet Laureate of West Tisbury

"Informative and fun to read—this book highlights the kinds of folks our special Vineyard culture invites to live here..."
   —**Ann Howes,** Master Painter and Artist

Acknowledgments

I thank many people who contributed to the creation of this book. The subjects of my interviews in *Part II* were incredibly generous with their time and prolific in telling of their passion for Martha's Vineyard. Sincere thanks to Suzan Bellincampi, Allan Keith, Janet Messineo, Peter Boak, Vicky Hanjian, Alison Shaw, Mary Grasing, Elaine Eugster, Isaque Silva, Debbie Phillips, Dave Medeiros, Terry Appenzellar, Kim Lawrence, and Jim Newman.

Special thanks to my husband Dan, for his patience in reading and re-reading my work, and to my very generous friends and relatives who gave me their insights and feedback.

A final thanks to the Vineyard for its cosmic qualities. It is a place where people can walk new paths, dream new dreams, and, yes, make an island home.

Elaine Pace

Foreword

Part I of this book tells of my transition from family life in New Jersey to full-time life on Martha's Vineyard. I describe the seasons and tell of "the real Vineyard," the one experienced by those who make a commitment to build a life here.

Part II tells the stories of fourteen others I interviewed—men and women of different ages, professions, and lifestyles who also made a deliberate choice to make Martha's Vineyard their home. Because they weren't born on the Vineyard, they are lovingly termed "wash-ashores." They are ordinary people, not rich or famous media magnates.

In selecting my random sample of interviewees, I focused on certain criteria. Most spent a significant period of their lives engaged in active careers and activities very different from the kinds of lives lived by Vineyard folks. They have settled on Martha's Vineyard year-round for a minimum of six years and, in some cases, for as long as thirty years. Their homes stretch across all the island towns, from Aquinnah to Oak Bluffs to Edgartown. They come from different parts of the United States and even foreign countries. Some came thinking that they would leave but never did. What vortex drew them to this island, seven miles off the mainland of southeastern Massachusetts? Their stories are emblematic of the richness and diversity of those who have chosen Martha's Vineyard as their island home. So why did they come? They agreed to answer that question in interviews with me.

"Why do they stay?" is the question addressed in *Part III*. And, in the end, what do these "wash-ashores" contribute to the island of Martha's Vineyard?

The new ferry, Island Home

ISLAND HOME

Introduction

A clear blue sky and a balmy winter day foreshadows a jubilant commissioning of the new ferry *Island Home* on Saturday, March 3, 2007, in the town of Tisbury on the island of Martha's Vineyard. Only a spattering of hardy boats dots the Vineyard Haven harbor during this winter season, but, ashore, a crowd of hundreds toasts the *Island Home* with invocation, speeches, and song. During the summer months, such a crowd isn't unusual, as the population of Martha's Vineyard swells annually from eighteen thousand year-round faithfuls to more fickle July and August crowds of one hundred thousand. But this day is different.

"Heart," says a man wearing jeans and carrying a child on his shoulders. "Look at this crowd. This place has heart."

"And history," another comments.

"Years. This took years," a third adds.

Each phase of the design and development of the *Island Home* had been debated at the Steamship Authority's drafting tables and captured conversation at post offices, stores, and work sites around the island. The *Island Home* is the tenth ferry to have carried passengers and vehicles between Woods Hole and the Vineyard. The ferries sustain the life of the island.

"We don't need a new ship," chimes an earthy-looking sixty-year-old whose hair was clasped into a ponytail of gray hues. "Our ferry *Islander* is fine."

"No, it's time," his swarthy partner contradicts as he stamps dried mud from his boots.

"It'll just bring more people to the island. We're growing too fast."

"The ferries are our lifeblood, like it or not. They're not just for summer tourists. They connect us with the rest of the world—supplies, food, medical care, employment. Some folks ride them to and from work every day."

"I still like the *Islander*."

But today isn't about the *Islander*. Today is a tribute to the future. The thirty-three million dollar *Island Home* carries twelve hundred passengers and seventy-six cars. Among those passengers and cars are a certain few who have chosen to make the island of Martha's Vineyard their home. I am one of those people.

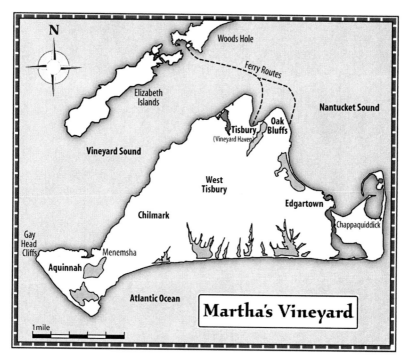

The Island of Martha's Vineyard

Table of Contents

Part 1
The Island as My Home

Seals and Serendipity

The ebony heads of two harbor seals draw a crowd to the edge of the shore at Long Point on a summer day in July.

"Seals, seals," a child exclaims. "Look, Daddy."

"I see them," the father replies. "They're not afraid of us. Sometimes they come in close enough to swim right beside us."

I remember the summer day when that very thing happened to Jeff, our son-in-law, visiting from Upper Dublin, Pennsylvania. A golfer and a suburban sort of guy, Jeff's eyes widened as Tanya, our daughter and middle child, shouted with the same excitement as the child who shouts today: "A seal, Jeff, a seal is swimming right beside you." Jeff turned abruptly and with evident anxiety, but momentarily his features relaxed and the anxiety was gone. "Oh, my," he said, "Oh, my."

Since we made our home on this island, my anxieties too have lessened. I remember the shoulds and coulds and woulds and how such words drove me in my earlier life. It took the first five years of living on this island to learn to act according to my feelings and values and not according to the values imposed by others.

The anxieties created by the rules and standards and expectations of others wash away like the prints of sandpipers along the shoreline. Finally, I can enjoy the life and the wisdom of a sixty-something woman who traveled a great distance to reach this point in her life. Not that it was easy. It never is.

Walking the shoreline along Chappaquiddick Island

Remembering the Past

I recall how systematically our family packed each summer for the trek to the Massachusetts shore. New summer swim suits, balls, kites, bikes standing tall on the roof of our station wagon, a book about sand castle design, the card game *Uno*, boxes of food staples – baked beans, spaghetti, peanut butter, jam, soaps and shampoos and laundry detergent and sunscreen numbered eight to forty-five. Each person, two adults and three children, had two individual towels, one for sunning and one for drying off. The cottage came with bare beds, so we filled another box with sheets and pillowcases and of course our personal pillows.

Overstuffed boxes sat on the porch just outside the kitchen door, waiting for Dan, my husband, to arrive home from work and tend to car patrol. He claimed the packing of the car as his special job, the culmination of days of planning and packing on my part and the children's. His special job was punctuated, however, with exasperated sighs, with sound effects like a low cryptic whistle, and with words such as "Whew, can't you folks learn to be more efficient? Do you really need all this stuff?" Attaching the bikes to the roof capped the drama. Since a roof rack once came loose from our car and sailed across a major highway in Connecticut, thankfully with no casualties, Dan was especially cautious about roof rack security.

At last the station wagon was ready, awaiting only the children. We negotiated the right side, the left side, and the middle of the back seat flanked with car games and books to read along the way. Ryan knew that the ocean would be on our right as we drove through Connecticut, so he relegated that spot to his sister Tanya for the first part of the trip. That was OK with her, as she loved to be on the right for the ride over the Tappan Zee Bridge in New York, with its distant view of the Empire State Building and the city skyscape.

Rebecca whined, "Why do I always have to be squished in the middle?"

"Because you're a peanut," Ryan replied.

"I am not a peanut. Mom, Ryan called me a peanut," the youngest child complained with puckered face.

Tanya, always the conciliator, jumped in, "Tell you what, Rebecca, I'll switch with you halfway."

"OK, but it's still mean that Ryan always calls me a peanut," she pouted.

All this for a week of vacation. We could only afford a week then. I saved all year for that week.

The family years unfolded like the sections of a carefully pressed cloth napkin. With few wrinkles, the napkin lay open before us. No more unfolding to do. Our three "children" were off to college and to graduate schools and the employment that no longer requires the financial support of parents. Here was an opportunity to create a new and different chapter in our lives.

Mapping Our Way

Mapping our way to Martha's Vineyard was serendipitous. For twenty-five years, I had worked as a teacher and an administrator in the field of education. On a pensive December Sunday in the year 2000, I opened the *New York Times* and saw an ad for a principal of a K-8 school on Martha's Vineyard. I had grown up in Massachusetts. Two of our three children had settled in Boston, and my mother, nearing ninety years old, lived in Lexington.

"Is this ad a sign or a coincidence?" I asked myself. For many years we had dreamed of living near the ocean. Here was our chance. Six months later, I accepted the job as principal of the West Tisbury School. For the first year, I lived with Tory, our family dog, in a small rental house near the school.

The rest followed as inevitably as a Slinky toy makes its determined descent down a stairway. Dan, my husband of thirty-five years, found a job designing drug trials for a pharmaceutical firm in Cambridge. He moved into a small studio apartment in the Davis Square section of Somerville. Every weekend he commuted to and from Martha's Vineyard on a Cape Air plane. I picked him up at 7 p.m. on Friday evenings and returned him to the airport on Monday mornings at 6 a.m. With this regimen in place, we sold our New Jersey home, bought a house on the Vineyard, and worked full-time for three years.

"How's work?" I asked Dan one weekend in 2004.

"Demanding," he replied. "How about you?"

"Demanding for me too."

During the first year of my principalship at the West Tisbury School, Massachusetts Governor Romney cut thousands of dollars in school aid. The reverberations of that cut affected class size, teacher security, and long-held practices and traditions in my school. Taxpayer watchdogs complained bitterly about rising school costs. I had left my job as superintendent of schools in a northern New Jersey town because that job, too, was more about business and finance than about education. I felt trapped in the same vise.

"We've created a facsimile of the lives we left behind in New Jersey," I said to Dan. "We decided to change the quality of our work lives, but that just hasn't happened."

"You're right," he replied.

Our jobs had become our identities. People knew me as a principal, not as a person. At last we mustered the courage to say, "Enough. We needn't be defined by our jobs any longer. It's time to live the next stage of our lives." Martha's Vineyard was the gateway.

Our decision to become "regular people" rather than "professionals" was daunting at first. We were just "Elaine and Dan," not "Dr. E" or "Dr. D." We felt the way our college kids had when they left home and began the creative process of defining who they were in a new setting, a new society, a different world from that in which they had been sheltered and familiar. Our decision took some courage and a lot of faith, but the rewards followed. We awaken now each morning where the sun rises and sets earlier. At night the skies dance with the stars of a place far from city lights, a place where Jupiter courts Antares and where the constellation Orion marks the seasons. Within five minutes we can be at the ocean, on a bike path, or deep in a wooded trail.

"Do you sail?" some people ask.

"No."

"Do you fish?"

"No."

"Why'd you come to the Vineyard?"

"To build a new life now that our children are grown and gone."

Some folks grimace and mutter words such as "Sounds weird. You left all that you knew to come to a strange place?"

Others say, "Wow. Congratulations. Are you glad you did? Was it hard? Do you think I'd like it here?"

"Depends," we reply.

"Depends on what?"

"Depends on a lot of things."

A gnarled oak tree at Cedar Tree Neck Preserve, North Tisbury

Retirement

Depends first on whether you and your spouse like each other. Retirement was more of a surprise than the departure of our last child for college. We remember the new freedom to work as late as our jobs entailed, with no obligation to make a family dinner or pack lunches or get the kids off to school and sports or check homework or do six weekly loads of laundry or be sure that everyone gets to church on Sundays. Unlike other parents we knew, we weren't sad when the children left. We missed them but read enough Kahlil Gibran during the 1960s to know that our children are our gift to the world, not our possessions or our protectors. Once our children were gone, we supported their life victories vicariously and offered advice when we could. They did just fine without us. But how would we do?

Through years of marriage and family and job obligations and the daily busy-ness of our ordinary lives, we realized that we had paid little attention to our relationship. We subordinated "us" to all those other demands. Would we learn to live together effectively again without the diversion of children and jobs and bills to pay and appointments to keep?

"Retirement? I never want to retire," some say. I feel sad for those people because, while retirement, like moving to an island and to a new culture, entails huge adjustments, those who don't retire may miss a world of discovery. Discovery about other people and places. More important, discovery about themselves.

We discover that we are poorly prepared to inhabit the same space for twenty-four hours each day without the diversion of our jobs and appointments and other obligations.

"Where's my coffee pot?" I ask early one morning.

"What coffee pot?"

"The green coffee pot I always use," I reply.

"I thought we'd switch to the Gevalia one."

"Why?"

"I don't know. I just like it better."

"Well, I like the Krupps."

"All right. We'll use them both. I was going to switch to decaf anyway."

The two coffee pots of the new retirees sit side by side on the countertop.

"Dan, I can't find the bread knife."

"What?"

"I can't find the bread knife," louder.

"I'll be right there, Elaine." He comes downstairs from the den where he is using my computer.

"Here it is."

"Why is it there?"

"I put it there when I emptied the dishwasher last night."

"The large knives go into this drawer," I point with unmasked annoyance. "The small knives go there. How do you expect me to prepare dinners when you've switched my utensils all around?"

"Calm down, Elaine. Cool it."

Now I am angry. "You make dinner," I storm as I exit the room to check my e-mail.

"Wait," he says, "I'm using the computer for a while."

"I told you to get your own computer," I say, teeth clenched.

"I didn't want to spend the money."

"I need my own computer, Dan."

During the first year after I left my job in West Tisbury, I took a publications job in Boston, but technology made it possible for me to work from home. When articles arrived from various authors, I was required to edit them immediately to keep the workflow going and to make our publication deadlines. The computer *tete-a-tete* continued for about a year. Finally I purchase a second computer.

I say all this now with a smile. Other new retirees assure me that our experience isn't unusual. I am happy to report that we now operate in the kitchen, and elsewhere, with remarkable synchronicity. We even share the same car.

Confinement

Whether or not you learn to love more than the magnificent scenery of the Vineyard depends upon whether it becomes a place of enterprise or of solace or of confinement.

"I haven't been off the island in five years," one woman proudly announces in the produce aisle at Up Island Cronig's Market. She wears carpenter's jeans and a tool belt.

"Two years for me," her friend remarks as she sorts through organic lettuce.

I think back only a few years to my ninety-mile round-trip daily commute westward in New Jersey and how, on weekends, we would drive twenty-five miles eastward in the opposite direction to enjoy a museum or a concert or a play in New York City. Or, we might drive an hour north to hike in High Point State Park or perhaps travel thirty minutes south to eat at a restaurant in Montclair. If anyone had ever told me that I would be seven miles out to sea and living on an island only twenty miles long and seven miles wide, I would have laughed in disbelief. But here I landed.

Would I want to leave the island only once in five years, two years, one year? No. Not for me. We don't feel trapped. With organization and good planning, the ferries move us off the island and back on again with little fanfare. Some people use the Bonanza buses to reach Boston. Others park an extra car in Falmouth. That's what we do. We visit the Museum of Fine Arts, have dinner in the North End, or cheer for the Red Sox at Fenway Park. Providence is equally accessible when we need a shot of city life. During the wintertime, busloads of islanders travel together to enjoy the Boston Symphony, flower shows, and other off-island outings.

The longer we live on Martha's Vineyard, though, the less inclined we are to worry about being confined. The confinement turns out to be delightful, especially during fall and winter and springtime. When the summer temperature is ninety degrees in Boston, it is eighty degrees here; when it is thirty degrees there in the winter, it is forty degrees here. The invitation of empty bike paths, the smell of fall hay, the lure of the off-season shore, and the friendliness of our unpretentious neighbors are a salve unimaginable in our former suburban lives.

A hidden trail waiting to be discovered

The Shoulder Seasons

It is a crisp October day. The grasses on the dunes have turned gray. The meadows are auburn. The leaves along the local roadways are just beginning to change color. We live in a frost bottom, so our leaves turn to yellows and ambers later, clinging to the trees long after other island trees have gone barren. We smell smoke. The Trustees of Reservations are conducting a burn in meadows nearby. These burns control growth and promote healthier vegetation. A trip to the post office to pick up our mail turns into a ninety-minute event because we meet and chat with friends along the way.

"What shall we do today?" Dan asks. Remembering years of indoor office and classroom and lab work, we have promised ourselves to exercise outdoors as often as we can.

"Let's take a hike."

Within this geography of less than 140 square miles, our menu of walking options is extraordinary. We may venture westward to the Fulling Mill Trail that surprises us with ocean views camouflaged by leaves in the summertime. On a different day, we skip over to North Road and wind through Great Rock Bight to a public Land Bank beach that sits on the Sound at the foot of a steep precipice. Or we walk from our house to Sepiessa and trail along the inlet, past magic fields that change texture and hue with each hike. We may visit Cedar Tree Neck, where we wind through forest, over streams, along the ocean, and around the perimeter of a small peninsula with dramatic drops to the ocean waves thrashing the rocky shore. On another day we walk through the maze of Felix Neck trails, and, with luck, we spot a red-tailed hawk along the way. One of our favorite local treks leads us to the south shore, to Long Point and its cobalt ponds and meadows that turn from gray to burgundy as the seasons change. "Will we swim in Long Pond or in the ocean today?" we ask ourselves. We swim comfortably in the Gulf Stream waters into October. On another day we wander southward a bit further past Quansoo and to Lucy Vincent Beach, empty now except for a few faithful dogs and their masters. If we were fishermen, we would enter the annual Bluefish Derby in September or wait eagerly for scalloping season in December. If we were farmers, we would mow and bale the hay in our fields.

"Let's kayak today," I say one May day.

"Ok."

We take our kayak and stop at Stonewall Pond for a quick paddle en route to Moshup Trail and the Aquinnah cliffs, changing color with every season and every weather condition. Though these cliffs have been memorialized many times in film and paint, we can't resist adding another picture to our own digital collection of photos. We catch a shot just as the lighthouse beam meets our lens. We recognize that the cliffs have eroded significantly in just the few years since we have arrived on the island. On the Vineyard we get a firsthand look at the power, the beauty, and the whimsy of nature.

Rock sentinels guarding a shoreline

Wintertime

"But what about the wintertime?" some ask. "Isn't it dreary?"

"Not at all. It's serene, not dreary. The bright blue summer skies mellow into pearl hues and we are reminded to mellow a bit, too."

Dan and I aren't bored when the summer season is over and the year-round residents have time again to socialize. Clubs resume, board meetings return to more regular schedules, and potluck suppers connect the community throughout the wintertime. The local Conservation Society, the Trustees of Reservations, and the Land Bank sponsor trail walks every Sunday. Clad in hooded sweatshirts and hiking boots, groups of twenty or thirty explore trails and properties not open to the public during the rest of the year. Intellectual pursuits—book clubs, art and writing and music programs, play reading, political debate—sharpen minds and sometimes tongues as well.

Issues that were suppressed or ignored during the busy summertime re-emerge to engage spirited discussion and debate. Six towns, six school systems, six sets of selectmen, and an energetic populace raise their Vineyard voices:

"Are chickens and guinea hens a public nuisance in a residential neighborhood? Or are they emblematic of the West Tisbury agricultural community in which they reside?"

"Should the annual Oak Bluffs shark tournament continue next year with its bloody shark carcasses on parade along the harbor?"

"Are our properties assessed equitably? Or should the rich or the summer-only residents pay more?"

"Should the dunes destroyed by a recent storm be rebuilt or

The tranquility of a winter road

should we let Chappaquiddick residents accept the path of nature and find other routes to enter and exit their special island adjoining our island?"

"Where and when and how can we provide affordable housing so that young families and workers can remain on the island?"

"Should we build a rotary at the Barnes Road intersection?"

"Can we install a red light at Five Corners in Vineyard Haven?"

"Do we limit the maximum speed limit to forty-five miles per hour?"

"Is the airport commission during its job? Do we increase air traffic to promote business or do we treat the increase of air traffic more conservatively?"

"Do we allow a contractor to develop the land he has purchased? Or do we honor the longtime residents who oppose new construction?"

"Without using chemicals, how do we maintain the health of our ponds as vegetation stifles them?"

"Will Sengekontacket Pond be closed to shell fishing?"

"Will the purchase of our local hospital by Mass General be an asset, or will it limit local control?"

"Should a waterfront resident be permitted to build a rock wall to protect the erosion of his property if that wall can cause increased erosion to neighboring properties?"

"Was it really a bunch of rowdy goats who were responsible for the destruction of the interior of a home in Chilmark?"

With passion and fierce democracy and humor, the issues go on and on.

Summertime

Off-season life is filled with local color, but nothing matches the dynamism of summer, like it or not. Islanders mutter interesting epithets about the influx of summer tourists around the Fourth of July. Still, the panoply of activity is the lifeblood of local businesses and entrepreneurs.

Tranquil island roadways become obstacle courses. Drivers learn to dodge confused itinerants, shaky once-a-year bicyclers, dreaded moped drivers, and sightseeing buses that stop frequently to share island lore. An elderly man talking on a cell phone backs out of a space at the Net Result Fish Market parking lot and smacks into a carload of hungry clam seekers in Vineyard Haven.

Hand-crafted chairs ready for tourists

In Oak Bluffs, Circuit Avenue is deadlocked. The Edgartown Triangle is impassable, especially on rainy afternoons when everyone goes to Stop & Shop for provisions. A Park and Ride bus eases the crunch by transporting people in and out of town. Even tranquil West Tisbury entertains a traffic jam near Alley's General Store and on Farmer's Market or Artisan Fair mornings. There's not a parking spot to be found in sleepy Menemsha. At the end of Waldron's Bottom Road en route to Long Point Beach a sign says, "Lot full."

Some folks vacation on the Vineyard only once. The absence of outlet stores, malls, boardwalks, and artificial amusements represents too extreme an adjustment during vacation week. "Nothing to do on a rainy day," they say. "How many times can you ride the carousel in Oak Bluffs? We're not into art galleries."

Others make a week of vacation an annual vigil. We meet such a family, two parents and two teenage daughters, at a Ben Taylor concert.

"This is our twentieth year vacationing here," the parents tell us. "We come from Franklin, Massachusetts."

One bemused woman says, "Each year we think it may be our last. But each January, in the throes of New England winter, we call our Realtor and book once again."

Theirs was our story too—a single week of vacation only once a year—a dream that one day we'd have more. Only when we were willing to relegate our old lives to the past and to risk trying something dramatically different were we able to create our island home. Sometimes we have to pinch ourselves to realize that now we live year-round on a beautiful island surrounded by the ocean.

But what of the rest of the people who lived their lives in other cities and suburbs and nations and yet who also chose this

Black-eyed Susans herald the season

island as their home? Why did those people, those who were not born here and who in many cases had no family here, decide to come? It is no secret that living on an island has its perils: isolation, expense, inconvenience, and the challenge of being an outsider in a place inhabited by natives whose family roots are as deep as the centuries are long. The stories of these "washashores" contain a bit of whimsy, a lot of faith, a little luck, and a yearning for something better, more meaningful, in their lives. Read on.

Part II
Others Who Chose the
Island as Home

Suzan

Keeper of a Sanctuary

"I want to be an old Vineyard salt," says the wisp of a woman whose drive is inversely proportional to her height. Her long curly hair, her broad smile, and her petite figure don't fool those who know her. This woman is a dynamo. "Martha's Vineyard is beautiful, stunning," she says, "but I wouldn't come here to wait on tables, no matter how beautiful it is. I need a mission."

Suzan visited the Vineyard a few times after graduation from Rutgers University in 1992. With a degree in environmental science, she worked as an environmental consultant. Subsequently she joined the Peace Corps. From 1993 to 1995 she served as a forester and an educator in Niger, West Africa. "I was part of the old Peace Corps. I lived in a mud hut in a village where tribal people with scarred faces sharpened their teeth. When we needed water, we went to a well. We took nothing for granted. Two years of this taught me the power and the justice of nature. If it didn't rain, the villagers didn't eat. That was that," she said.

"Returning to America was overwhelming. I had trouble transitioning from life in a mud hut to a place that offered six hundred different types of cereal."

Suzan found a job on a schooner and, for the next three years, lived on a boat in Bivalve, New Jersey. *The A.J. Meerwald* was a restored oyster schooner—a teaching ship. "I got up before the sun and went to bed shortly after dark," she tells me. "I shared a bunkroom with others. Some mornings we'd get up at 3 a.m. to catch the tides." Suzan was approaching the age of thirty, still a wanderer. She knew she wanted to do more with her life than to catch the tides at such an early hour.

"Since college, I realized I was energized by estuaries and tidal flats—intricate systems—enchanting wildlife," Suzan tells me. "So I took three weeks and crafted an estuary tour from New Jersey to Florida and back. I visited wetlands, searched for places with fisheries and fishing cultures and historic little main streets, and ate local shellfish. By the end of that tour, I knew that I wanted to return to environmental work in an ocean community on the East Coast. I'm about an avocation, a passion. I live to work, not work to live.

"The next step was easy," she says. "My parents owned a summer house on Martha's Vineyard. They subscribed to the *Gazette*. I opened the paper and saw the ad that called my name: *Environmental Educator Sought to Work for The Trustees of Reservations on the Island of Martha's Vineyard.* I realized I had changed a lot during the past ten years," Suzan says. "I wasn't seeking new horizons like a young college graduate or a retiree. The past decade cemented what I knew I wanted to do with my life. This was it. In 1999, I was hired. I had learned that no job was worth it if it didn't align with my values. This one did. It was worth the sacrifice and the outrage of paying $2.69 for a jar of peanut butter when I could get the same jar for $1.99 off-island.

"I was saved from 'the Vineyard shuffle,' seasonally moving from one rental place to another, only because my parents owned summer property. For three months, I lived in a shed on their property. It had no plumbing or electricity. After that, I lived for the next seven years in housing provided by the Trustees. I was lucky. Like so many others in their thirties and forties, there was no way I could afford to buy a house on Martha's Vineyard. I couldn't even afford to buy my father's house when he sold it," she admitted.

"During my time with the Trustees, I was promoted to become the statewide director of training. Later the Trustees

Suzan at Felix Tree Neck Audubon Sanctuary

wanted me to relocate. 'Nope,' I replied. 'Either I do it from Martha's Vineyard or I don't take the promotion.' Reluctantly, they agreed."

I ask Suzan why she feels such commitment to the Vineyard. "I renew myself again and again," she says. "Each winter I try to learn something new. I've learned to knit, to keep bees and chickens, to gather my food, to fish and rake for oysters and clams. I have a self-sufficiency based on simplicity. I know I can do those things in a small town in Vermont or New Hampshire or Maine," she says, "but I've developed a community here that shares my values. I love to open the phone book and to find one or two people I know on every single page."

In 2006, Suzan found a new job, one with housing that gives her a backyard of 350 acres. She became the director of the Felix Neck Wildlife Sanctuary, a Massachusetts Audubon Society property. "I hear barn owls screaming by the light of the moon," she exclaims. "It's phenomenal."

When I ask Suzan about her fears for the future of the Vineyard, she says, "On the first weekend when I came to the Vineyard, I learned how cool it was to have a beat-up old bike or a run-down cottage near the ocean. Today people are building bigger and bigger homes, McMansions. We don't need bigger and bigger anything—we need small and simple and meaningful lives. I want us to try to hold onto the values that make this island such a unique and amazing place. I, for one, am going to do my best to make that happen."

☙

Suzan

Suzan Bellincampi *grew up in the suburbs of New Jersey, then spent two-and-a-half years as a Peace Corps volunteer in Niger, and four years sailing aboard a restored oyster schooner, where she conducted environmental education. She arrived on Martha's Vineyard to work as an education coordinator and later a director of training for The Trustees of Reservations. She is currently the director of the Felix Neck Wildlife Sanctuary. She lives in Edgartown with her chickens, bees, and honey.*

Allan

Ornithologist

Imagine a red-haired boy of ten wandering all over summertime Chilmark a half century ago, climbing hills, exploring old roads, and riding horse trails to the neighboring town of West Tisbury through fields and farmland and all the way to the south shore beaches. The boy winds past stone walls built a hundred years earlier and past fields that have gone fallow, promoting the growth of small trees ten feet tall.

The boy returns to Martha's Vineyard every summer. (He says that he spent some time on the Vineyard every year for each of the next fifty years.) He swims at Menemsha, fishes for flounder off the jetty there, and dives into the channel searching for lost fishing sinkers. He bodysurfs at Squibnocket and other south shore beaches. As an adolescent, he loves the sweaty square dances of Saturday nights accompanied by the live music of two fiddles and a piano.

"We boys all tried to swing the girls off their feet in the Virginia Reel," he recalls. "The musicians played for three hours. Allemande left and do-si-do and dive for the oyster or dig for the clam became so familiar that eventually the caller was hardly needed. Tim Carroll's father was the caller then. The square dances were held in The Tavern located next to the Chilmark Store, but only soft drinks were served there. At 10 p.m. when the music ended, the group of teens headed to Squibnocket Beach where we collected enough driftwood for an hour-long bonfire. We talked and sang until 11 p.m., when I was expected home. We had no alcohol, no drugs of any kind. We were naïve and innocent," the man reminisces, "Those times were wonderful."

Allan is that young man. He was born in Boston, grew up in Brockton, and worked in New York City. He spent thirty-seven years of his adult life raising a family in a sleepy New Jersey town named New Vernon. It was his fortune that, in the spring of 1946, on a gray day with little wind, he accompanied his father on a Vineyard visit to walk the land of a farm for sale in Chilmark. There were no farmers in Allan's family. One grandfather had been a banker, the other a shoe manufacturer. Neither was his father a farmer, but he did like duck shooting, and that was the attraction of the Vineyard in 1946. Allan recalls that only two five-acre fields were fully cleared on the property of seventy-five acres, and a gigantic rock, a glacial erratic thirty feet long, twenty feet wide, and nine feet high sat stubbornly on one section of the land. His father bought the farm and had that rock dynamited. Its pieces were added to the jetty in Oak Bluffs, where they still sit today. Agnes Flanders, a neighbor, told Allan years later how, as a girl, she liked to climb up on that rock and sit on the top. Allan recalls his own pleasure sliding down the snow-covered rock in wintertime.

"That was an old Chilmark joke," Allan says smiling. "My father got money for selling rocks!" But for Allan, the stones on the property presented a new challenge each year upon his arrival in early summer. Once he grew into adolescence, his father insisted that he and his brother "work the farm." One of their annual jobs was to lift from the fields all the rocks pushed up by the frosts of the previous winter. "Between the two of us, we could lift stones that weighed one hundred fifty to two hundred pounds," he remembers. "We used crowbars and shovels and towed behind the tractor in what we called our stone boat. We picked up all the rocks turned up by the plow. We added many of them to the stone walls nearby. Once in a while, we'd find an Indian arrowhead. I learned to drive a tractor before I was allowed to drive a car.

"My father hired Ozzie Fischer, who turned ninety in 2005 and lives at Beetlebung Corner, to run the farm. He and his family were allowed to live on the property. He knew everything there was to know about farming," Allan says. 'You do whatever Ozzie directs you to do.' There'll be no questions about any of it, my father said.

"So we cut the field for hay, and Everett Whiting baled it into bales two feet long, eighteen inches wide, and a foot thick," Allan says. If the spring was good, with reasonable rain, three hundred to three hundred fifty bales of hay came from the big field. We'd pick them up, stack them on a flatbed trailer, take them to the barn, and heave them into the hayloft. The job took all day, even with the help of Ozzie's four kids, his brother Arnie, and Phil Spaulding.

"And that wasn't all," Allan says. "Have you ever tried to weed a carrot patch? Few things are more frustrating and more time consuming than trying to get out the weeds while not disturbing the new carrots. As a reward, Ozzie and I ate warm tomatoes right off the vine. We kept a salt shaker in the stone wall of the vegetable garden to season those tomatoes and eat them right there.

"Fourteen hundred baby chicks arrived on the farm every springtime. They were kept in two chicken houses with heaters, and we had a large hen house for the chickens that laid eggs. Ozzie and I killed, picked, and dressed lots of chickens," Allan tells me. "We sold them to the Menemsha Market and the Chilmark Store or to people who came directly to the farm house to buy eggs. At the end of the summer when the tourists left and business died down, we'd keep one hundred fifty to two hundred pullets on the range. When the weather got cold and they had to come in, we'd sacrifice the remainder of the laying hens and keep the pullets to grow over the winter. With a couple of roosters, the cycle continued the next summer.

"We also had pigs that we butchered for sale at the local market. All except Chester, of course. Chester was a magnificent boar who always got the $50 first prize at the county fair."

I ask Allan if the farm had any other animals during the 1940s and 1950s. "We had six dairy cows and twenty-three white-faced Hereford beef cattle," he replies. "We supplied milk to the Cooperative Dairy, a local enterprise that collected milk from many private farms. The bulk of the dairy's supply came from Elisha Smith on the Katama property where the Farm Institute now stands. We sold our milk cows when H.P. Hood & Sons brought pasteurized milk to the island and sold it for less than the dairy could.

"I remember a great perk we had while we had those cows," Allan continues. "We had our own milk separator and you could make as much heavy cream as you wished. We made it so thick that a spoon could stand up in it. I carved my mother a long-handled spoon out of wood and we used to scoop cream right out of the bottle. Sure tasted good on raspberries.

"The last thing we did was to raise white-faced Hereford beef cattle. The Herefords were sold at the live animal markets in Boston. On the island, though, the Portuguese community was one of our favorite customers. At the end of the summer, they roasted beef on a spit as part of one of their annual feasts.

"We raised enough hay to get the dairy and the beef animals through the winter. We had a trench silo where we created silage with the most wonderful smell because it had citrus rinds in it. I can still smell that fragrance."

Allan speaks of his father Eldon with great pride. "He didn't know farming," he says, "but he read every book he could on the subject. He bought textbooks on grass, on crop rotation, on the development of milk animals, and on other aspects of farming.

Allan, off to the woods with his binoculars

We introduced contour farming to the fields. It was a demonstration project for the agricultural extension service and for the Ag Society.

"Those early years infected me," Allan confesses. "I knew I had to return. I prayed that Winkie, my wife, would learn to love the Vineyard as I did. I wanted to return and retire here."

In the meantime, Allan graduated from Harvard Business School, majoring in finance, worked in New York City and in Princeton, and supported his wife and family of three children in New Vernon. "I picked New Vernon because it was rural," he says. "I felt sorry for suburbanites whose only experience of the outdoors was mowing a lawn. I liked New Vernon because it was an active farm community. I became a selectman there and tried to help pace its progress. I was the only selectman with any farm experience."

When I asked Allan about his biggest fear for the future of the Vineyard, he replied, "I've seen more growth on the Vineyard in the past five years than I saw in New Jersey during the thirty-seven years I lived there. I support the concept of an Island Plan," he goes on, "but, honestly, it's the kind of people who move here and live here who will govern the rate and quality of change."

"So what's the best thing about the Vineyard?" I ask.

"Conservation efforts are promising," he replies. Again he speaks with pride of his father's foresight. "He owned seventy-five acres of prime land with ocean views," he admits. "He could have made millions selling it to a developer. But he loved Chilmark, and he didn't want to change the nature of the town. His land had grown so much in value that he no longer could afford to pay the estate taxes. Instead, he gave the property away—some in conservation easements to the town of Chilmark—another part to his three children. My wife and I saved for seven years until, in 1992, we could build our own house on that gifted parcel of land, and that's where we live today. My dream has come true. I've returned, this time for good."

Allan

Allan Keith retired in 2000 after a career in investment management services. Educated at Amherst, Harvard, and Yale, he studied zoology as well as business. Ornithology became his lifetime passion, and he authored or co-authored three books and published over thirty articles and reviews. Allan served as an officer or a trustee for the U.S. Council for Bird Preservation, the New Jersey Conservation Foundation, the New Jersey Audubon Society, the American Birding Association, the Polly Hill Arboretum, and the Martha's Vineyard Chamber Music Society. He is co-author of Island Lives: A Catalogue of the Biodiversity On and Around Martha's Vineyard. Allan and his wife Winkie live in Chilmark. In 2008, they celebrated forty-four years of marriage.

Janet

Fisherman and Taxidermist

Janet was a fisherman long before she held a rod and reel. She fished for many years, trying to find a place where she felt comfortable and hopeful about life. Her small frame housed a huge heart and the drive to take her across the United States and back to Martha's Vineyard, where she found her home.

"I remember the exact moment I knew I could never stay in Salem, New Hampshire," she tells me. "I was brought up Catholic, with all those rules, and my parents were factory workers. My mother was an English war bride. As a teen, I sold hot dogs at the racetrack and worked in the shoe factory over the border in Lawrence, Massachusetts. I knew I didn't want that life. I remember the day I realized it.

"I worked on the assembly line gluing toes on shoes riding down a conveyor belt. Two women worked across from me—a mother and a daughter. We had a raffle at work. Those two women won a trip to Bermuda. 'We can't go,' they said. 'We have to work.'

"That did it! I punched out that day and never returned. It was the Sixties. People were traveling all over the country. I made my way to Cape Cod, thinking I'd find a job in Provincetown. I didn't like it there. But I met two men with a Vespa, and they asked if I wanted to go to Martha's Vineyard.

"'Where's that?' I asked.

"'It's an island,' they replied.

"I had never heard of the place. I thought of palm trees and ocean breezes. 'Sure,' I said. 'I'll go.' In those days I blew in whatever direction people pushed me.

"I remember walking off the ferry and up Union Street," Janet tells me. "Connie Sanborn's store, Bare Essentials, had a display of brightly colored clothing and feather boas and fun clothes for young people. I wanted to be a free spirit and an artist. I felt at home and safe right away. I spent the summer meeting people—never did get much of a job. I got food wherever and slept by the drawbridge or under a rowboat or with friends. For a while I found work on a fishing boat in Oak Bluffs. I got fifty cents or a dollar a day to bait hooks and do other small jobs. I met George Lawrence.

"'Where're you from?' I asked George.

"'Medford,' he replied, 'but I didn't want my boys to grow up in the city. I brought them here, but I need help. I'll give you room and board if you help me to cook and clean and care for my boys.'

"I said, 'Sure.'"

It was August. George and his boys were African-American. She thought nothing of it. But one October day two policemen knocked on the door when George was at work and the boys were in school.

"You got $10?" the policemen asked.

"No."

"Then you're a vagrant. You'll have to get off the island or we'll arrest you."

Janet describes her helplessness, her fear. (She explains that it wasn't until many years later that she realized that bigotry had something to do with the policemen's actions. She was an eighteen-year old white girl living with a black family. "At the time, I was clueless," she confesses. "I just wasn't aware of social judgments.") While waiting for the ferry, she called a friend who drove her to New York City. "I met more people there, just hung out, then went off to Chicago," she explains. "We hitchhiked or found rides with others we met. By March I wanted to return to the Vineyard. I did just enough cleaning jobs to save money for a one-way plane ticket. I thought I was so worldly, but I would've gotten into terrible trouble if I stayed in the cities. I was naïve and saved by the skin of my teeth."

Janet returned to the Vineyard, but not for long. She met Butch, and her wanderlust continued. "We went to New York City, we hung out. When we wanted to come back to the Vineyard, we knew Chief Maciel would arrest us for co-habiting. That was a crime in those days. We came up with the perfect solution. On the corner of Lexington and Twenty-Ninth Street, Butch asked me to marry him. We found a justice of the peace and learned that we couldn't marry in New York without parent permission. We were only eighteen.

"So we hitched to North Carolina," Janet says. "We could marry at eighteen there. People weren't nice to us—we were hippies and all—we were from the North and it was the South—but then once we were married and legal, everyone was great. The marriage license cost five dollars, but the JP gave us our money back and wished us luck.

"We made our way back to the Vineyard as a legal married couple. His dad taught history at the high school, and his mother, Mary Hayden, was wonderful to me from the moment I showed up on her doorstep married to her son."

Still without a rod or a reel, Janet continued to "fish" for her self. She and Butch wanted to be part of the Haight-Ashbury scene, landed in San Francisco, and lived in a commune. Finally she returned to New Hampshire, where her parents took them in. "Occupations weren't important," she tells me. "We did whatever we could just to survive—I waitressed and worked in a factory; he made candles. We did flea markets for a while. We saved four thousand dollars and bought forty acres of land in New Hampshire. We lived in a teepee, cleared the land, built a log cabin, raised our own vegetables and rice, and did our laundry in the pond. But by the end of 1971, I wanted to come home, not to Salem but to the Vineyard. I wanted to go bowling at the bowling alley in Tisbury, and, most of all, I wanted to eat a hamburger!" Janet's return to the Vineyard ended her first marriage.

When she returned to Martha's Vineyard, this time for good, she got a job at the island hospital during weekend hours. "I felt so cool in my hard hat," she exclaims, "I did flashing on the roof. Then I started working as a waitress at the Black Dog Bakery and then the Black Dog Restaurant from 1972 to 1976. For the next four years, I worked at Helio's Greek Restaurant, where I served John Travolta and Beverly Sills. Can you imagine it! The restaurant was near the Nobnocket Garage, owned by James Taylor. The garage turned into an artworker's guild—artists like Travis Tuck and Julie Mitchell and Thaw Malin were there. I reminded myself that I wanted to be an artist one day."

Janet writes regularly for *On the Water* magazine. A chapter is dedicated to her fishing expertise in the 1988 book *Reading the Water* by Bob Post. She is featured too in David DiBenedetto's 2003 book *On the Run,* in which he describes fishing with Janet in his journey from Maine to Georgia. But I still had heard nothing about her being a fisherman.

"So when did you become a fisherman?" I ask her.

"I never fished in my life," she replies. "But in 1976 I bought a rod and reel for my boyfriend. He wasn't using it. I wanted to try it. I lived on Beach Road right next to the Lagoon. I begged people to teach me. Once it rained, and I didn't even know whether it was OK to fish in the rain or whether I should just go indoors."

Janet's voice becomes markedly more animated. "Fishing saved my life," she tells me. "It's my passion, my spirituality. Everyone has a gift. Mine is fishing. I got hooked and became compulsive about it. I never wanted to be a good *woman* fisherman. I just wanted to be a fisherman. Tim White and Jackie Couthino taught me techniques that had been passed on for generations. I'm a bass fisherman. I love the nighttime. I love the solitude. I fish from shore and go wherever the bass are—Tashmoo, West Chop, Cedar Tree Neck, Pilot Hill Farm.

"One wintertime a friend invited me to spend a few weeks at Satellite Beach in Florida. I was excited to go. She lived two blocks from the ocean, but when I went out at night to go fish on the beach, she said, 'You can't do that here! You'll get killed. It's not safe. A woman alone in the dark. Forget it.' That's when I realized how lucky I am to be on the Vineyard. I've never been frightened by anyone, even late at night. The more obscure the beaches, the better I like them. Breaking into the world of bass fisherman couldn't have happened to me anywhere except on the Vineyard. Once I had a dream that a big bass was waiting for me at the Edgartown Bridge, and I woke up my boyfriend to drive me there to fish alone in the middle of the night. Rats ran all over the beach, and the night herons screeched and scared me. I caught my fish and hunched in a corner under the bridge until morning when he came back to pick me up. That's how hooked I was.

"I met my husband Tristan in 1985, a year after I won second place in the shore division for striped bass. My fishing partner Jackie took first place. It was the last year striped bass was in the tournament—there was no bass in the derby for the next nine years. I wanted that fish preserved, but I didn't like the fiberglass method of taxidermy. I wanted to use the skin of the fish. With Tristan's encouragement and a loan of two thousand dollars from my father, I left the Vineyard for three months in 1987 to learn taxidermy at the Pennsylvania Institute of Taxidermy. Tristan took care of my house and my dog.

"A year later, Tristan and I were married at the Christiantown Chapel. All our parents were there. We were forty. We've been married twenty years now. We adopted a two-year-old Wampanoag child who is nearly finished with high school now."

Meanwhile Janet practiced the art of *taxidermy* that she learned in 1987—not the fiberglass method but taxidermy with real skin mounts. She explains that the word taxidermy has its origins in the Greek words *taxis* (to move) and *derma* (skin). The ancient Egyptians embalmed fish as well as humans, and sometimes placed embalmed fish in the burial vaults along with the remains of important deceased people. Attempts to preserve creatures are noted as far back as recorded history.

"The job of a taxidermist is challenging," Janet says. You try to preserve these miracles of nature in as near a lifelike form as possible. A fifty-pound fish sometimes takes me a year," she says. "I'm such a perfectionist. I get a deposit but I don't get the rest of my pay until the fish is done. My workshop is in the basement of our home, but once I even taught the West Tisbury School kids how to do taxidermy in an after-school program. I think the kids' taxidermies are still hanging in the assistant principal's office. Once I did a fish for Spike Lee. I did others for Jim Belushi, William Weld, Charles Ogletree, and Bill Clinton. I even did a crab that went to the White House. Fish that I have mounted are hanging on walls in thirty-six states in the nation and also in China, Canada, and England. I'm the only taxidermist on this island. Everyone knows me. There's a special joy in working with Mother Nature's original and perfect art.

"You know what?" Janet goes on. "*I* finally became an artist too. I started creating wildlife sculptures and now they're being shown in three island galleries. Can you believe it! My newest venture is doing shore charters where I teach people, mostly women, how to fish. I guess I lived my life backwards. I didn't find my niche until I was nearly forty years old, but now, move over baby, I've got work to do!

"I live in the most magical place in the world, not because of the beaches and the sunsets, but because I've been free to be myself, to find my passion and to become a fisherman, a taxidermist, and now even an artist and teacher. Life can't get any better than that."

Janet putting finishing touches on her taxidermy

Janet

Janet Messineo *has lived on Martha's Vineyard since 1966 and fished the surrounding waters for over thirty years. She graduated from the Pennsylvania Institute of Taxidermy in 1987 and currently owns and operates Island Taxidermy and Wildlife Art Studio in Vineyard Haven. Janet is the president of the Martha's Vineyard Surfcasters Association and a member of the Martha's Vineyard Striped Bass and Bluefish Derby. She is a regular columnist for On the Water magazine, and she has been featured in other publications such as Robert Post's* <u>Reading the Water</u> *(1988) and* <u>On the Run</u> *by David DiBenedetto (2003). Janet lives in Vineyard Haven with her husband Tristan and their son Christopher.*

Peter

Musician and Teacher

"Why do we have to go home?" the boy pleaded with his mother. "Please, please, let's stay."

"If we don't go home," the mother replied, "we'll not be able to return next year."

Peter knew his manners, so he didn't retort, "But if we don't go home, we won't have to return!" Those were his thoughts every single year as he and his family departed from the Lagoon Heights cottage of his grandmother to return to life in Basking Ridge, New Jersey. He recalls saying a private goodbye to the *Islander.* "I'll be back," he whispered.

Aunt Sally, Peter's great-great aunt, acquired the Oak Bluffs cottage in 1904 as payment for a debt. His grandmother ran away from her New Jersey home at the age of eleven. Her mother had died, and she was not happy with the stepmother her father married. Aunt Sally raised her into adulthood. She, his grandmother, and his father made the imprints of the footsteps that he followed many years later.

"I loved that two-week summer vacation," Peter tells me, "but my grandmother didn't believe in free rides. Our day began with chores: Feed the birds, water the window boxes, help prepare lunch or dinner, do laundry. Then off to the Lagoon we went until lunchtime. An hour of quiet time came next. The children were required to find a quiet place for an activity that required no talking. I often read. But the moment the hour was over, off to the Lagoon we went again 'til suppertime. Those days were magical.

"The nights were too. I slept on a cot in a bedroom with my

brother. My bedroom had windows on three sides. In those days the sailing camp was run by the Massachusetts Girl Scout Council. I fell asleep to the sound of 'Taps' ending the Scouts' day. The sound of the bugle wafted across the lagoon and right to my bedroom. It was such a pure sound, especially on nights with no wind and perfect calm.

"Our two-week vacation wasn't complete without two special outings. On the morning that I awoke to find picnic baskets stuffed with ham and cheese sandwiches and oatmeal cookies, I knew it was South Beach outing day. From the moment we spread our blankets on the sand, we rode those Atlantic waves for the rest of the day, stopping only for a quick lunch.

"On another morning when I found towels and blankets and beach supplies, I knew it was Gay Head day. We couldn't wait to feel the clay squishing through our toes as my brother and I climbed the Cliffs. We didn't know much about protecting the Cliffs in those days. We didn't need to pack food for Gay Head day because little Mrs. Greider had a Quonset hut on South Road along the way. She ran a diner with wonderful chowder and grilled cheese sandwiches. The diner helped support her after her husband died. He was the lighthouse keeper. Lunch was always at Mrs. Greider's place. The Quonset hut is still there.

"Down the lane from my grandmother's cottage Lillian Chignell lived. She was a former governess from England. Chiggy lived in a pre-fab Sears and Roebuck house that stood behind a huge glacial boulder in her front yard. My brother and I climbed that boulder and sat there to enjoy the tea and cakes she prepared for us. For many years Chiggy cooked on a kerosene stove outside with her pots and pans hanging from the trees. That tiny, tiny lady, barely four feet eight inches tall, lived to be 103!"

Peter tells me that he always loved music and his grandmother provided him with piano lessons as a child. "The piano was great," he admits, "but the organ was so much more exciting. I began to play the organ at ten years old. By thirteen I had decided that I wanted to be a church organist for my career."

"Are you sure?" his grandmother asked. "Can you make a living doing that?"

Harold Heeremans provided the answer. Professor of music at New York University for many years, Harold played the organ at the Union Chapel during the summertime. "I sat next to him every Sunday and turned his pages and learned how he led the musicians and directed the quartet. He was my mentor. One Sunday, after church, my grandmother marched me right up to him," Peter says.

"This boy wants to play the organ for his career," she told him. "You tell me if he's talented enough."

"Play for me, Peter," Harold invited.

So Peter did.

"He has the talent," Harold told the grandmother.

And so that Vineyard organist set the course that Peter followed for the rest of his life—but not on the Vineyard, at least not yet.

Ten years later Peter graduated with a degree in music education from the Westminster Choir College in Princeton, New Jersey. Moving to Lafayette, Louisiana, he taught for a few years before choosing a career as a church organist there. Eight years later, he settled in Dallas, Texas, to work on a master's degree. In 1984 he returned to Summit, New Jersey, to serve for ten years as minister of music at the Central Presbyterian Church. The church had seven choirs and twelve hundred parishioners. Peter worked from 9 a.m. to 9 p.m. on many days, as he was responsible for all the choirs and services, including weddings and funerals. Nearly thirty years of his life had passed since Mr. Heereman's pronouncement. He couldn't be working harder, but something was missing. He decided to take a sabbatical.

"I wanted to experience the Vineyard in the wintertime," he says. "My summer memories were so poignant."

The winter scenes moved Peter just as much. "The setting was peaceful, idyllic," Peter says. "The community was so welcoming. It felt natural and good to be here. That little boy voice that had told the *Islander* that I'd return, said, 'You don't have to go home this time. You can stay.' I arrived on January 2, 1994; by March 2, I decided to remain. I wrote letters to the churches to tell them that I could be a substitute organist, but the Vineyard had other plans for me.

"The Nathan Mayhew Seminars were in full swing in those days. These seminars offered adult education on topics of interest. I took an office job there and soon was working with Elderhostel orchestrating island tours. They were themed," Peter tells me. "One tour might have the theme of ecology, for example, and I'd find speakers from the Land Bank and the Preservation Trust. If the theme were about the arts, I'd book visits with artists and authors and painters. The work was interesting and integrated me more into Vineyard life."

Peter grew confident that he could indeed make a living on Martha's Vineyard. He took a job at the Edgartown Bank in the mortgage department and later as the head of operations there. "For the first time in my life, I wasn't employed as a professional musician. I learned I could do other things. Wanting so much to live on the Vineyard freed me to use a new part of my brain and develop other parts of myself. I realized that I had skills I didn't even know I had."

Peter conducting a rehearsal of the All Island Community Chorus

Simultaneously people were recognizing Peter's talent. He soon found himself directing the community singing of Handel's *Messiah* at the Grace Episcopal Church, an annual tradition. "People told me they wanted to sing all year-round. That was the start of the Island Community Chorus. By 2007, the chorus had grown to include 125 singers and three annual concerts. We have many donors that keep the organization going. During the past few years, we've even had an anonymous donor whose contributions enabled me to bring professional musicians and soloists to some of our performances and to expand our music library. The Vineyard is a very diverse place, but music is a language that everyone understands."

Peter works now as a music teacher in the Tisbury School. "Working with young people has made me think more and more about the future of the Vineyard. I want us to be gracious and welcoming to outsiders but I fear that we will collapse under our own weight if we don't find some way to cut down on traffic during the summertime. Our roads and air quality won't tolerate more trucks and tour buses and automobiles and mopeds. It's the American mindset," he says. "Everyone wants to have a vehicle. The VTA (Vineyard Transit Authority) has done a fabulous job with its buses, but we must find creative ways to do more."

Peter ends with a wry smile: "Despite all the change, I can

still find the solitude, the special paths and trails, the Vineyard byways that energize me. No day is ho-hum here."

Peter

Peter Boak made his permanent home on Martha's Vineyard in 1994 after completing a career as a music teacher in Lafayette, Louisiana, and a full-time church musician in Summit, New Jersey. He works currently as a vocal music teacher at the Tisbury School, as the minister of music for the Federated Church in Edgartown, and as the director of the Island Community Chorus. He shares his expertise by collaborating in local theatrical productions and serving philanthropic organizations. *The Peter R. Boak Music Award is given annually to a graduating high school senior who plans to pursue a career in music. Peter resides in Oak Bluffs with his Great Dane Maisie and his feline companion Hoboken.*

Vicky

Minister and Lifelong Learner

Seven months pregnant with her second son, Vicky first saw the Vineyard in 1964. Friends had told her that Martha's Vineyard was a great place to camp, so she and her husband Armen booked two weeks at Webb's Campground. "There was no store at the campground then," Vicky tells me, "no flush toilets, no showers.

"Ruth Webb sat right at the front entrance in an old beach chair. Every morning she'd compose a new poem about the weather on her manual typewriter and tack it up in the outhouses. In those days there were no flush toilets, no showers, no store. But Webb's, with its pine needle floor and primitive as it was, was the nicest campground we had ever camped in.

"What did I know about the Vineyard before that first camping stint? Nothing, absolutely nothing," Vicky confesses. "I had never heard of the place.

"And it rained every single day of that first two-week vacation! I can still see the World War II bunker that sat on the beach at Katama, its steel reinforcing rods inviting our sons to climb it year after year until it faded away with the shifting of the ocean tides year after year. The fog was amazing. It settled in, muting life's stresses like a heavy snowstorm and shutting everything else out."

Vicky continues: "I cried when I had to leave. I didn't know if we'd be able to return."

Indeed they did. They camped at Webb's every single summer from 1964 to 1977, when they finally were able to build a log cabin on a parcel of land Armen found in Oak Bluffs. During their campground years, Vicky and Armen learned about the phenomenon of year-round residents having to move out of their homes and into the campground during the summer so that their houses could be rented, providing money to pay mortgage and taxes. "The shuffle" still happens; Vicky tells me some people must move every time the rent increases, not just in summertime.

"People think of Martha's Vineyard as a land of rich and plenty, but economic survival is a brave art for many," she says. "Yet that's what I love most about the place. It's real.

"My favorite island scene is the view from the drawbridge coming from Oak Bluffs into Vineyard Haven. The morning light is almost surreal as it hits the white hulls of the sailboats and reflects off the homes of East Chop. Then come the oil tanks and a working shipyard where people repair, build, and refurbish— that's a reminder that nestled within all this beauty are workers. The water scene is awe-inspiring and sacred, while the subculture works behind the scenes to keep that sacred scene looking as it does. That's the magic of the place."

Vicky supports the farming subculture through CSA, community supported agriculture, a movement that has spread across America. She and Armen buy shares and are then entitled to a weekly visit to Whippoorwill Farm or to Thimble Farm to pick beans, sugar snap peas, shelling peas, cherry tomatoes, mixed greens, whatever is seasonally available. Farm picking starts in springtime. "Some years are sparse at first," she admits, "but by August I fill three large shopping bags overflowing with giant heads of red-leafed lettuce"—"works of art," she says— along with tomatoes, squash, potatoes, carrots, onions, bok choy, watermelon, orange and magenta zinnias, purple and pink and white chrysanthemums, and a weekly allocation of eight sunflowers.

The farm is subsidized by the financial contribution of local people who believe that food sources should be close to home. But community visits to the farm provide more than food, Vicky realizes. "Look at this one," she hears an excited child call to his mother as he pops up from the strawberry patch clutching a fat, red strawberry. "That child is learning that strawberries don't come from green boxes covered with cellophane," Vicky says. "It's easy to romanticize these weekly jaunts to the farm fields, chatting with neighbors, returning home with food to eat and flowers to adorn the tabletops. But, after spending thirty minutes, stooped, picking strawberries in full sun, I realize the plight of migrant workers who spend eight hours every day laboring in similar fields with no bounty to take home to their families, no flowers for their tables, only their meager seasonal wages. Where else on Martha's Vineyard would you see two men in a field picking beans and talking about what it means to be a survivor? There are many 'survivors' on Martha's Vineyard."

After the weekly farm visits, Vicky goes home to her log cabin. "I know I'm home when I smell the pine," she sighs. "Our home has no negative energy. When we built it, we used only wood, no plastic. We had always lived in parsonages," she explains. "This was the first time we had our very own place. There was no need to scrub and paint and clean and layer what others had used before us. The house is simple, small, and safe. It measures only twenty-four feet by twenty-six feet, but it supports us. It doesn't sap our energy or our funds. It helps us stay committed to a life of voluntary simplicity. If we consider bringing in something new, we ask first what can be eliminated.

"The awe of the place is in what's outside the house," Vicky tells me as she recalls a scene on State Beach during her first year of full-time Vineyard life. "We walked near the edge where the waves lap the shore, when I hear a barking sound. Turning around, we see a harbor seal plopping along on the beach. We turn and approach it until we are less than six feet away. The seal freezes for a moment, its barking ceases. In the eyes of that seal we see the wisdom of the universe. Then the eyes gaze toward the

Vicky at the door of her log cabin home

ocean, its flippers flap the black body off the sand, and it returns to its source in the water. 'Another miracle,' I said to Armen."

Vicky describes what she calls a spiritual quality she sees in some of the people she meets on the Vineyard. "There's a symbiosis between the beauty of the island and the response of the people," she says. We're honored to have met some of those who made the history of this island—Herbie Hancock, the Larsens, Robert Norton from Lambert's Cove, Franklin and Norman Benson, salt of the earth people who told us of fish and farms and delivering milk in a wagon. Theirs is the energy that permeates the place, not the hyper-energy of the summertime that so many identify as the essence of the Vineyard. This island is an organism. I can hear it exhale at the end of the summer as the Vineyard people resume their ordinary but blessed lives.

"We will live longer here," Vicky assures me. "We live productive lives filled with service to others, but we find time for yoga, for walks, and for meditation, luxuries we never had in our New Jersey lives. You know, I never did yoga before I moved here." She tells me that two of her three children have decided to move to the Vineyard, too, even though economic realities relegates one of them to become part of the Vineyard shuffle. "Now we are real grandparents," she acclaims, "not event ones, the kind who arrive only to celebrate a birthday or a holiday. Our family life is stronger than ever. We find ways to sustain each other. We all must find ways to sustain this precious island."

☙

Vicky

Vicky Hanjian is a retired Methodist minister but still preaches intermittently at some of the island churches. She serves as a volunteer bereavement counselor for Hospice of Martha's Vineyard, and assists that group, too, as a member of the quality assurance committee. She volunteers at the Island Food Pantry, filling twenty-five bags each week with grocery items and fresh produce for food pantry clients. She coordinates the adult education study group at the Chilmark Community United Methodist Church. She is studying Hebrew and active, too, in the community of The Hebrew Center of Martha's Vineyard. Vicky and her husband Armen are residents of Oak Bluffs.

Alison

Photographer and Artist

It never occurred to Alison that she would end up living year-round on the island of Martha's Vineyard, or that she could, in her wildest dreams, make her living as an artist. All she did was come to the Vineyard for the summer, after graduating from Smith College in 1975. And then she never left.

Smith College was nurturing and a welcome antidote to the anonymity of a large public high school in Bethesda, Maryland. "My childhood was a happy one," Alison tells me. "My mother was a professional photographer, but she gave up her career so that she could raise a family. When I was ten years old, she taught me to load film onto reels and to work in the black and white darkroom in our basement. During the summertime, I visited my grandparents, Alma and Chester Van Tassel, who lived on South Water Street in Edgartown. They introduced me to Ruth Appledoorn Mead, the grand dame of the Old Sculpin Gallery. Each summer, I took painting lessons from Mrs. Mead. Only because I had rigorously trained as a painter did she allow me to exhibit my photographs there during subsequent years.

"My Vineyard summers were wonderful," she continues. "My family and I spent sunny days at the Chappaquiddick Beach Club, where we had our own cabana. We sailed whenever we had a chance. My brothers Stephen, Michael, and I fished with drop lines from the town wharf, and we sold seashells and other beach treasures from the front porch of 'Pinkletink,' our family cottage on Dunham Road. We picked raspberries in my grandparents' back yard and walked through the woods out to Green Hollow to visit cousins. On rainy days we rode the Flying Horses at the

Carousel in downtown Oak Bluffs and ate popcorn at Darling's on Circuit Avenue.

"When I was eleven, I got my first job—I gave tours at the Thomas Cooke House at the Dukes County Historical Society in Edgartown for two hours a day. During the afternoons, my grandmother served tea in her living room. In the evenings, my grandfather donned a sport coat and tie and his sneakers, and my grandmother put on a silky floral dress and a lightweight sweater, as the family gathered at the round table in the Water Street dining room. Grandma, who was very short, would slide down her seat, stretching her right leg to press the buzzer on the floor under the table, whence Bebe, the white-haired Irish cook who served our family for years, marched proudly out of the kitchen and presented the most scrumptious food. Who could imagine a better life?

"As I progressed through my adolescence, I had to choose whether I wanted to pursue painting or photography. Because high school and college yearbook and newspaper work were so compelling during those years, I chose photography but never dreamed it would ever be more than just a hobby.

"In college, when it came time to declare a major, I chose art history rather than studio art, since Smith had a very strong program. Being an artist just seemed so frivolous," she confesses, "and studio art didn't feel like a career at that time. I thought that with an art history major, I would be able to find a respectable job in a gallery or museum somewhere." After graduation, she applied for an internship at the Corcoran Gallery in Washington, D.C., but was turned down. Postponing an immediate decision, she and four Smith friends decided to spend the summer working on Martha's Vineyard. "Three of us still live on the Vineyard full-time today," she adds.

"I had to find a job," Alison admits, "but I was shy. I convinced a friend to walk with me into the office of the *Vineyard Gazette* and to help me ask for work. Dan West, business manager at the time, hired me as an inserter. I'd insert section C into section B and section B into section A. Manually collating, I'd make neat little stacks of twenty-five newspapers each—they'd be bundled and go out the back door for delivery. By the end of the summer, I graduated from being an inserter to being an addressograph operator, running a very temperamental machine that stamped the addresses onto the newspaper."

The five Smith women lived in a barn in West Tisbury behind the office of the old newspaper *The Grapevine.* Coincidentally, at the same time, Tom Mendenhall, the former president of Smith College, retired to the Vineyard with his wife Nellie. "I crewed for Mr. Mendenhall on his sailboat the *Louisa K. Fast,* and we took long walks at Cedar Tree Neck, where they lived. It felt like we all were continuing our college years together. Once that first summer came to a close, and my classmates and I realized we weren't at all ready to move back to the 'real world,' some of us decided to stay for 'just one winter.'

"The first winter led to another summer and then another winter and then another summer until finally I admitted that I had created a home here," Alison says with surprise. "It seemed so unreal. Like living in Disneyland."

Settled on Martha's Vineyard, Alison hadn't yet realized that an artist could indeed make a living there. She started taking pictures for the *Gazette.* "My first news assignment for the Gazette was to photograph the Marcus House on Chappy. The architecture was ultra modern for the era, and it was considered inappropriate on the landscape. My pictures were intended to show how architecturally out of scale it was. I loaded my film at night in the stairwell of the West Tisbury barn where we lived, and processed it in the kitchen sink. I volunteered to teach photography at the

Edgartown Boys and Girls Club in exchange for the use of its darkroom where I printed my photos."

Alison with one of her newest photographs

Alison expresses the awe she feels for the shorelines of the Vineyard. "The place where the land meets the sea has such emotional impact for me," she explains. But she also believes that the man-made aspects of the Vineyard contribute in a significant way to its beauty. "Look at the gingerbread cottages in Oak Bluffs," she points out. "They were built around the same time as many of the whaling captain homes in Edgartown. Look at the farms of West Tisbury, the stone walls set against the open spaces in Chilmark! Aquinnah stands alone, being defined primarily by its natural, non-man-made environment. I believe that, with common sense and appropriate regulation, man-made development can be responsible and good for our community. I love the open spaces, but I love the neighborhoods too. I know there has been some controversy in recent years about cramming yet another house in every vacant lot or nook and cranny in Edgartown. I actually think these new houses contribute in a positive way to the streetscape, that the flow of the houses, one beside another, enhances the feeling of neighborhood.

"Getting by over the years wasn't easy," Alison tells me. "As was the case with many young people committed to making a life for themselves on the Vineyard, I did some creative house shuffling. I could take you on a tour of the houses I have occupied since deciding to live year-round! At my grandmother's unheated summer cottage on Dunham Lane, I spent considerable time in the kitchen with the oven door open to get heat. I also lived for a while in Bill Black's camp behind the dump in West Tisbury—it had no electricity—we had to start up a generator every morning to pump our water. When I finally decided to buy my own house in 1979, only four listed houses fit my $30,000 budget." Alison ended up buying a run-down house in Oak Bluffs, where she still lives today. But even home ownership didn't alter the need to move seasonally. For a number of years during the winter she rented her house to a carpenter in return for some fix-up jobs it desperately needed, and she house-sat for Walter Cronkite. "Can you believe that Walter Cronkite didn't have a working TV?" she laughs. "If you wiggled a button, you could get poor reception on only one channel."

Alison describes the renaissance of the Arts District being developed in Oak Bluffs. In that district is the new Alison Shaw Gallery, a bright haven filled with the hues of light and color that make her photography so appealing. Alison and her partner, Sue Dawson, own and run the gallery, and have worked as a team with Alison Shaw Photography for the twenty years they've been together. During her thirty years of life on Martha's Vineyard, Alison learned that an artist can indeed make a living, but her fame followed sacrifice, commitment, and a strong belief in herself.

"The Vineyard gave me the gift of being able to earn a living doing what I loved to do," Alison says. "I loved the creative life, worked at it, and eventually people began to see value in my photography. Many people hate the summer crowds, but those summer people helped me to earn a living and enabled Sue and me to support a family together. I'm grateful, too, to have my studio, my children's school, and my home within a five-minute walk of one another. Only on the Vineyard!"

જ્જાજી

Alison

Alison Shaw is a fine art and editorial photographer. Over five thousand of her original fine art prints are in public and private collections worldwide. Her work appears regularly in Yankee Magazine, Martha's Vineyard Magazine, and Cape Cod Life. Her photography has distinguished diverse publications such as Henry Hough's essays, Remembrance and Light, Images of Martha's Vineyard; Until I Saw the Sea, children's photos and poems; Vineyard Harvest, a cookbook; and Finding Martha's Vineyard, a celebration of the African-American community on the island. Alison has taught photography workshops in Tuscany, Mexico, Nova Scotia, Maine, New Mexico, and Martha's Vineyard. Her gallery, Alison Shaw Photography, is located in Oak Bluffs, where she lives with her partner Sue Dawson, her daughter Sarah, and her son Jesse.

Mary

Lover of Animals

"Your friend lives in a tree house on Martha's Vineyard?" asked the sixteen-year-old.

"Yup," her sister replied. "She's a free spirit."

"I'll say. I'd love to see it."

"Why don't you come visit, Mary?" invited the sister.

"I will," Mary replied. This was the first time she had ever heard of Martha's Vineyard.

Mary arrived on the Vineyard in 1974 and visited the tree house located down an unmarked, overgrown jungle-like path near Lucy Vincent Beach in Chilmark. Onto the limbs of an oak tree someone had placed two windows between a crude wooden floor and an equally rough-hewn roof. A rocking chair sat next to a stream nearby. At night Mary camped in Lambert's Cove. Only ten days on the Vineyard convinced her that she'd return.

Mary had completed her junior year of high school near Marillac, Illinois. Families in her town worked for the wealthy in nearby Glencoe. Mary admits that she felt the same sharp socioeconomic contrast when she arrived permanently on the Vineyard. "My sister did errands for Katharine Graham," she said. "But I felt comfortable that there were people here just like me."

Mary returned from that first Vineyard visit determined to move herself to Martha's Vineyard. She spoke with a young newlywed couple she met through a Pentecostal church in Oak Bluffs. With the impatience of youth, she begged them to take her into their Tisbury home.

"I'll clean your house and run your errands," Mary promised. "Please let me come."

The couple needed her help and served as an intermediary between Mary and her parents. "My parents weren't crazy about the idea, but they let me go," she admits. "Besides, I had already called Northbrook High School and had my records transferred."

Mary never returned to Marillac. Early in her senior year, a man who was a deacon at her Pentecostal church began to pursue her. Three months later, she was married. She graduated from Martha's Vineyard High School and had her first child, Gabriel, in November of 1975. Her second child, Tabitha, was born in 1977. The Pentecostal church pitched in when the babies were born. The young woman who eagerly came to the Vineyard to see a tree house had inadvertently made the island her permanent home. A mother of two infants, she stayed at home and lived a placid life, introducing the children to daily walks at Cedar Tree Neck in North Tisbury, along Lucy Vincent Beach in Chilmark, and on the ancient paths of West Tisbury. "My kids spent half their young years in Edgartown at Felix Neck. I was drawn to that place from the start.

"The best part of Martha's Vineyard is the people, the community," Mary says. "I wouldn't have gotten here if that young couple hadn't let me live with them. Others led me onto new pathways. As the children grew older, I began to clean houses. Today I still clean the home of a man whose family I cleaned for twenty-four years ago. When my marriage failed, the families whose houses I cleaned gave me support. One, a lawyer, helped me to sort out the legal complications of being a single mother with little income. He designed a plan so that I could buy my share of the house where I still live on Main Street in Vineyard Haven. But, despite his plan, I didn't have enough money to complete the transfer."

"That simply won't do," said another house cleaning client. 'You deserve to have that house, Mary. I'll loan you the money."

"I paid back every cent," Mary says.

"I love my house," Mary continues. "It's one hundred fifty years old. It was moved from the Campground in Oak Bluffs. It has character. And I can reach the top of the kitchen cabinets even though I'm only five feet tall.

"I was an animal fanatic," Mary tells me. "In Northbrook we had dogs, cats, fish, gerbils, bunnies, and even a turtle. But my husband hadn't allowed me to have animals here. Once I was divorced, I yearned for a dog. I met a veterinarian on the island who told me about the National Education Assistance Dog Service (NEADS), an organization in New England that sought volunteers to train dogs to assist handicapped persons. My prayers are answered," Mary thought. She knew she couldn't afford to own a dog, but, if she volunteered to train a NEAD dog, all the dog's expenses would be covered. She traveled to Princeton, Massachusetts, to pick up her training manual and her dog, Wessie. The training went beautifully. Sadly, Mary let Wessie go off to her assigned home to work with her handicapped owner. Wessie had a seizure, making her incapable of continuing her work, and she was returned to Mary. In the meantime, Mary accepted a second dog named Keebler.

"Keebler's was quite a story," Mary says proudly. "She was a bright dog, graduated from my training, and was assigned to a high-profile woman with MS who worked in Maine. Keebler was often photographed with her owner, and the public in Maine began asking questions about the dog. NEADS responded, telling people that the organization had a long waiting list of other people with handicaps who needed a dog's assistance. As a result, an entrepreneurial Maine administrator devised a program called 'Puppies in Prisons,' using selected prisoners to train the NEAD

Mary and Wessie at Groomingdales

dogs. The program was mutually beneficial for the handicapped persons in need and for the prisoners whose work with the dogs assisted in their own rehabilitation.

"Acts of kindness gave me my first home on the Vineyard, my own house, and my first dog," she says. "When that Vineyard vet told me how I could get a dog through NEADS, little did he know that my work would open the door to an entire new prison program in the State of Maine. NEADS has grown into a national organization."

The generosity of Vineyarders continued to open new doors for Mary. She tells me how a friend encouraged her to do some part-time work at a small dog-grooming business called

Groomingdales. Groomingdales was then located down a rough dirt road near Chicama Vineyards in West Tisbury. To her surprise, she loved bathing the dogs there. "The next thing I knew," she exclaimed, "the owner was asking me if I wanted to buy the business!"

"I can't do it," she protested. "I don't have the confidence. I don't have the money. I can't."

"Yes, you can," the owner replied. "You can send me a percentage of the profits until the business is paid off."

Mary agreed and, within forty-two months, Groomingdales was all hers. She moved the business to her Vineyard Haven home, where it flourishes today.

"I'll tell you one more story," Mary says. "A man who brought his dog to be groomed every month liked to talk about his travels. One day he said, 'If you could travel, Mary, where would you go?'" She says that her answer was instantaneous. "When I was in the third grade, I learned about islands where animals weren't afraid of people. They were called the Galapagos. That's where I'd go if I could."

The next month the man arrived with his dog and a large packet of articles and travel information he downloaded from the Internet. "I drooled over those materials for two years," Mary tells me, "until I saved up enough money to do the trip. It was the year 2000. The place was as amazing as I'd dreamed. I try to go back every year when I can afford it.

"Nothing is accidental," Mary says. "A couple of years ago, I needed to hire a helper to work at Groomingdales. I interviewed twelve people and picked a woman who seemed perfect for the job. After I hired her, I learned that her family lived in the village of Puerto Ayora in the Galapagos! Now, when I go there, I stay with her family."

Mary describes the changes she has seen in Vineyard Haven. "The post office was in the Rainy Day building," she says. "The IGA store was located at the site of the current post office, Cumberland Farms was a tiny building where the Tisbury Marketplace is now. I've changed too. I've become self-confident. I've grown a lot. I walk in the West Chop woods every single day, and I think of all the dreams that the people of Martha's Vineyard have made possible for me."

෴

Mary

Mary Grasing still lives happily on Main Street in Vineyard Haven with her Lab Wessie and a frequent parade of dogs that are groomed or boarded at Groomingdales. She rides a friend's horse, Max, every week and helps with his care, and she continues to bike long distance for charity. Mary spends as much time as she can with her grandson Tyler whom she describes as "fabulous," and who lives nearby on Martha's Vineyard. She retreats each wintertime to the Galapagos, where she has established treasured friendships she describes as "reptilian and sea-going and Ecuadorian of the human kind."

Elaine

Humanitarian

To see Elaine bicycling around Martha's Vineyard today, you'd never guess that she was an unathletic college student, still living at home in Brooklyn, when a friend invited her to join in a bike trip on Cape Cod and the islands of Nantucket and Martha's Vineyard during the summer of 1956.

"Martha's Vineyard?" she asked. Is it really an island?

Her friend replied that indeed it was. "I know someone with a home in a pretty little town called Oak Bluffs," she said. "We can visit her."

"Sure," Elaine replied in a college student's cavalier way. "I'll go. I'll borrow a bike."

Elaine recalls her first impressions of the Vineyard. "At first I liked Nantucket better—it was a stark landscape with few trees." But she was impressed with the Vineyard light—"so bright, so different from what I was used to in Brooklyn."

Biking adventures and Vineyard exploration took a hiatus for many years until she and her husband Hans returned thirty years later to seek a vacation home. Both had been faculty members at Goucher College in Maryland for more than twenty years. Hans had visited the Vineyard and loved its ambiance.

"It was our spring vacation," Elaine tells me, "and pouring rain when we arrived on a Friday night. We found a room at the Vineyard Harbor Motel. Saturday morning we went to a Realtor who showed us an absolute shack in the recesses of Vineyard Haven. The shack sat on eight acres of land with a well, no running water or electricity, and an outhouse! But the land was wooded and magnificent.

"I couldn't even look at Hans," she confesses, "I just knew that he loved it too. We asked for the site maps and returned without the Realtor that Saturday afternoon to walk the property. We walked around the lot with the plot map. The ink ran in the rain."

Hans and Elaine returned to their Vineyard Haven retreat during each of the next four summers. "We planned a building project for each of those summers," she says, first a porch, then an addition for his three daughters. We built with our own hands." Elaine tells me that the days of hard physical work were a welcome change from their intellectual lives. During the evenings when their work was done, they relaxed with their college coursework, creating new curricula for the next year's teaching. Tragically, though, Hans died in 1987.

"I wasn't sure I'd ever return to the Vineyard," Elaine admits. Fifty years old and prematurely a widow, she returned to her familiar Baltimore life.

As exercise and therapy, a friend invited her to learn serious biking. By 1990, she was biking forty miles per day around the Baltimore area. She still couldn't bring herself to return to the Vineyard. "I decided to join the Peace Corps. I signed up to teach data processing in the Seychelles, a group of islands in the Indian Ocean. My assignment was to begin in August," she reminisces. She rented her Baltimore home for the two years that she'd be away, but the tenant insisted on moving in by the Fourth of July.

"Where shall I go for three months?" she wondered. The Vineyard was her answer. "It spoke to me," she said. Before she left for the Seychelles, she realized she wanted to return to the Vineyard to make her year-round home on the island whose lushness and light had so moved her nearly forty years earlier. "After forty years of teaching in the same job, I needed a change," she says. "At the end of my two years in the Seychelles, I moved permanently to the Vineyard."

Elaine relaxing after giving a talk at the Want to Know Club

One day, as Elaine rode her bike to explore new parts of the island, she discovered the Polly Hill Arboretum. Moved by its uniqueness and its beauty, she entered the visitor's center to ask if she could volunteer there. Barely had she completed her membership application when she began working in the visitor's center. "One day I biked there," she said. "A week later I worked there. You roll up your sleeves and offer to help, and you can make a little difference."

Elaine made a difference indeed. She joined Hospice, became president of the Friends of the Vineyard Haven Public Library, served on the board of the Chamber Music Society, and joined the Vineyard Committee on Hunger. "I may do this forever," she says. "The work of the hunger group supports the food pantry, Meals on Wheels, and national and international organizations that fight hunger—Oxfam, Save the Children, the Haitian Fish Farm project.

"My service life is supplemented by my intellectual life here," she comments. "I've met so many lifelong learners. Book clubs, poetry reading, play reading groups are filled with people just like me. I feel stimulated every day."

One of Elaine's favorite clubs is the Want to Know Club. Founded in 1893, this group of twenty women meets from October through April. Historically, many participants were wives of fishermen whose husbands were off at sea. At each of their afternoon meetings, twice monthly, the women hear a research report on a topic related to the designated theme for the year. "Last year's theme was mysteries," she tells me. "We heard reports on the Bermuda Triangle, on Edgar Allan Poe, on why birds sing. Fascinating. Each of us commits to doing one report every other year. In the interim, we host a meeting.

"The island is incredibly small and wonderful," she comments. "My closest friend is a woman I met in the garden club and also in a book club. One day, while chatting, we learned that we attended the same Brooklyn high school, and we were in the same graduating class! That's the difference between the Vineyard and my other worlds. You're not anonymous here. You matter."

⊙παπ୨

Elaine

Elaine Eugster holds a Ph.D. in the History of Science from Johns Hopkins University, a masters in mathematics from Yale, and a masters in computer science from Johns Hopkins. She taught at Goucher College in Maryland for forty years before her retirement in 2001. She serves as a Friend of the Vineyard Haven Library, a trustee of the Martha's Vineyard Chamber Music Society, and an ongoing volunteer for Hospice, Polly Hill Arboretum, and the Vineyard Committee on Hunger. In her "free" time she partici- pates in the Want to Know Club, the Garden Club, the Peter Luce Playreader's Society, a poetry group, and a book club. Elaine is a resident of Vineyard Haven and reports that her greatest joy is in the visits of her three stepdaughters and seven grandchildren every summer.

Isaque

Immigrant/Citizen

In his native city of Ipatinga in the state of Minas Gerais in southeastern Brazil, eighteen-year-old Isaque took an aptitude test that told him he should be a priest. Ipatinga was a rich city, with six major universities, steel mills, and a paper processing plant. The surrounding countryside was agricultural and scenic. Isaque was more drawn to farming than to the priesthood, so he earned a degree in agriculture. "Instead of tending a flock of people as a priest does," Isaque tells me, "I ended up tending a flock of animals. I worked on a pig farm—more than 5000 pigs. I checked their health every day. I took care of everything on the farm—other animals, fish, and crops too."

"Come to America," his brother Elio said. The year was 1989. Elio had lived on Martha's Vineyard for three years, first cooking at the Ocean View Restaurant, then running a coffee roasting business, then opening a vegetable store. "You'll love America," Elio told him. "We Brazilians work hard. You'll be successful."

"I followed my brother when I graduated from high school," Isaque tells me. "When you come to America from Brazil, you imagine you will find a giant city with unimaginable technology. I flew into Boston and spent a night there, then I came to the Vineyard. I was shocked. Here was countryside, a rural area, houses with wood-shingled siding, everything ordinary and basic. I loved it. I found it so elegant to live near the ocean. I never lived near ocean. Now I live on an island surrounded by water. It's amazing that I'm at this place. After you live here awhile, you understand why people want to keep it the way it is the way it is today. People keep it as simple as possible. Since I came in wintertime, I'd never see anyone on the street after 8 or 9 p.m. I imagine that it would have been even quieter a hundred years ago.

"I wanted to find a job right away. In Brazil, I worked since I was a young child. My father owned a supermarket, and my brothers and I all stacked shelves, made deliveries, and served customers. I think working is good for children. Many young Americans have too much time on their hands. Because we Brazilian children all worked during the daytime, we attended school at night from 7 to 11 p.m. We studied at night as hard as we worked during the day. We had to pass every single course, and we usually took eight to ten courses during a school period. If we failed even one, we had to repeat the year!

"For my first American job, I worked at the Ocean View with my brother," Isaque tells me. "Then in 1990 I started working for Warren Doty. I boxed and iced fish, but later I became the floor manager at Menemsha Basin Seafood in Vineyard Haven. I worked there until the business closed in 2003. From 1993 to 1995 I also tutored a Brazilian student at the high school. This tutoring was an important job because it forced me to improve— to learn to speak English as I do today. I can write it too. Then, starting in the winter of 1996, I began to drive an oil truck for Packer. I always had two or three jobs. I worked hard."

I ask Isaque to talk about being an immigrant and he mentions his gratitude to Warren Doty. In 1994, Warren, a Chilmark resident and selectman, sponsored Isaque in the long process to citizenship. "You have to have five years of permanent residence before you can become a citizen," Isaque tells me. "It's a grace period when you show you will be a good citizen. You prove yourself. You have no criminal record, and you study hard. I learned about the history of America and its independence in the Revolution. I studied the Civil War, the rights promised in the

Constitution, the presidents, and the meaning of the flag. I take the final test for citizenship in 2008."

Isaque on his daily rounds

Isaque tells me that he feels sad for the twelve million illegal immigrants in the United States today. "They provide cheap labor, but they hide and cannot be free," he says. "They need better programs to help them become citizens. They don't mind paying taxes because they get so much from living in America. I can only speak for the Brazilians I know, but every one of them wants to be legal and will do whatever it takes. As long as you behave, you get the freedom to work and get wealth."

"How does your ability to get wealth here compare to what you experienced in Brazil?" I ask Isaque.

"It's very different," he replies. "In Brazil, we earn less. We also do not buy a house unless we can pay for it in cash. We don't get mortgages."

"How did you get your home here?"

"It was the year 2005. Elio was at a junkyard looking for a part for a car. He met a man who had a place to sell in Oak Bluffs, just a shell. He asked the price and told me it was a good offer. I knew I could complete the shell and make it into a house. I went to the bank and got a mortgage and a construction loan. Today I have a beautiful home with two thousand square feet of living space," he says with pride.

I learn that Isaque has not returned to Brazil since a visit in 1999. "I have bills to pay," he explains, "and my wife Maria and my daughter Gabrielle to support. The trip is expensive. I miss my mother in Brazil. But I tell her stories so that she does not worry while she is so far away from me. I tell her people here aren't fearful of someone doing something weird to them—stealing cars, breaking into houses, walking away with their belongings. People don't lock their doors. When you tell that in Brazil, people don't believe you. People think I'm telling them a fairy tale."

"Is there anything you don't like?" I ask Isaque.

"Two things," he replies. "I don't like selfish people. I heard a man talking on the ferry. He complained because he had property worth ten million dollars and now the Land Bank lets people walk right next to his property. He is a selfish man. I am grateful that my wife can pack us sandwiches and we can picnic on that Land Bank property. This privilege is a precious thing to have. The second thing I don't like is when summer comes with all those people from the mainland—they have no respect—they don't know how to drive. It's hard to drive my truck in summertime. But I understand that we must earn a lot in a short period renting houses, selling souvenirs and services to tourists, and doing construction and landscaping. Still, I can't wait for October! Then, like the bears, we hibernate."

Isaque

Isaque Silva has lived on Martha's Vineyard for eighteen years. For thirteen years he served as a foreman at Menemsha Basin Seafood, and he has driven an oil truck for Packer's and Vineyard Propane for ten years. His brother Elio owns two local businesses: Fogaca in Vineyard Haven and North Star in Edgartown. His two other brothers remain in Brazil with his parents. Isaque lives in Oak Bluffs with his wife Maria and his daughter Gabrielle.

Debbie

Life Coach

Debbie's eyes sparkle and she becomes animated when I ask how she first saw Martha's Vineyard and why she decided to live here. She and her husband Rob moved here permanently in 2001, twenty-three years after her first romantic impression of the island. Meanwhile, she lived in Ohio, Iowa, and Boston.

"I first set eyes on the Vineyard on a rainy, foggy, cold September day in 1978," she tells me. "My husband and I were staying with my in-laws in Chatham on Cape Cod. His father was a Mayhew. Though his branch of the family had not inherited Mayhew land on the Vineyard, he was proud, nevertheless, that Mayhew Lane had been named after the family. 'Go see the place,' he urged us. 'You'll love it.'"

Debbie confesses that she was unenthusiastic about the outing. She remembers an article from *Rolling Stone,* telling how Carly Simon and James Taylor lived on Martha's Vineyard, and she recalled asking herself why people would want to live on an island.

"Can't we wait until the weather is better?" she asked, but they decided to go.

They rented mopeds, an activity she adamantly vowed never to repeat in the ensuing years, and they rode the roads along the ocean from Vineyard Haven through Oak Bluffs and into Edgartown. Amazing, she thought to herself, as they drove past the Inkwell and Sengekontacket Pond and State Beach and all the way to Katama. "This is where I belong," she exclaimed.

But life intervened. Debbie remained in Ohio and worked as a newspaper reporter until 1983. Knowing how enamored she was with her Vineyard dream, her boss, a summer Vineyard resident who subscribed to the *Gazette,* gave her his newspaper each week when he finished reading it. Photography was one of Debbie's special interests. She remembers following the story of the emergence of a new, young promising photographer named Alison Shaw. "Vicariously I watched her career unfold," Debbie tells me. The *Gazette* articles fueled her dream to return to the Vineyard some day.

In 1983, Debbie became the deputy press secretary to Senator John Glenn while he was running for the Democratic presidential nomination. When he dropped out of the race, she returned to Ohio and became the press secretary to the governor for the next five years.

In 1989, her marriage floundering, Debbie began to reassess her personal and professional goals. She wanted to attend the John F. Kennedy School of Government and earn her master's degree in Boston. In 1990 she graduated with a degree in public administration. Before her return to Columbus, she and her sister planned a Vineyard visit, Debbie's return to the island after twelve years.

"Everything I remembered about the beauty of the Vineyard was still true," she affirms. "I felt embraced, invigorated. I never felt that way about a place before."

Debbie returned to the Vineyard for annual weeklong vacations, staying each time in a different down-island inn and exploring the nooks and crannies of the Vineyard towns.

Back in Columbus in 1990, Debbie ran a nationally and internationally syndicated television show entitled "Life Choices." Within a few years, she realized that the career of life coach fit her perfectly. She loved helping others use their gifts, reach their goals, and realize the potential in their lives. She created a Vision Day, an opportunity for people to have an entire day to explore their goals. With the development of her first Vision Day, Debbie moved back to Boston in September 1996,

Debbie welcoming a client to a Vision Day

and she began regular Vision Day programs in 1998. "I'm a huge step closer to the Vineyard now," she thought.

In 1999 she met her second husband Rob and they established a joint business as life and executive coaches. "One of the greatest advantages of being a coach is its portability," Debbie explains. "We can design the business any way we want to do it. We design it so that people come to Martha's Vineyard for their Vision Days. They come from England, California, Michigan, Ohio, New York, Texas. They stay in the island inns, and many hike or bike the dirt roads and ancient ways of the island. Many clients return with family and friends."

Once they settled into their Deep Bottom home in 2001, Debbie and Rob scanned the February newspaper calendars to find events where they would meet local people and get an insider's view of island culture. She remembers a program presented by Kate Reilly, an animal communicator. Reilly, who had worked with many horses and other Vineyard animals, told their stories to a packed crowd in the Katharine Cornell Theatre in Vineyard Haven. Audience members listened attentively and questioned in earnest.

"I tend sheep," one woman lamented. "I love them and feel so sad when I must choose which to slaughter. What should I do?"

"The sheep know why they're here," Reilly replied. "Tell them it will be quick and painless. They're grateful for your love and care."

"How passionately these people care for their animals," Debbie thought.

She tells another animal-lover story, and giggles as she describes one day when she parked in front of the West Tisbury Post Office to pick up her mail. Every single car in a line of five contained a dog.

"There was dog as driver, dog as passenger, and dog as cargo," she tells me. "And in another car sat a bunny!"

When the driver returned to that car, Debbie asked her if the rabbit enjoyed the ride.

"He gets really mad if I go to pick up the kids at school without him," the driver replied.

Debbie adds that her years on the Vineyard have been filled with similar delightful scenes and interactions—quirky, charming, spontaneous.

She asks if we have time for just one more story that reflects just how unique this island is. "I was in Donaroma's Nursery sorting through flowers in a refrigerator and trying to create a fall bouquet of yellows and ambers and oranges. A woman with a deep and commanding voice tapped me on the shoulder and said, 'Darling, I want your opinion about these flowers and don't you dare lie to me.' I whirled around to see the striking figure of Patricia Neal. I offered my opinion about her flower choices and she reciprocated by telling me that I should reconsider my fall bouquet and buy pink peonies.

Then she departed. When I brought the fall bouquet to the register, the salesperson handed me a wrapped assortment of pink peonies as well."

"Don't ask," the salesperson said.

Debbie takes the flowers back to her West Tisbury home. "I love the Shaker shingles," she says, "and my outdoor shower. I actually have a client from Ohio who so loved my outdoor shower that she installed one at her house in Ohio! But most of all, I love the way my Vineyard home lets the outside in. We have lunch watching butterflies and hummingbirds and trying to figure out exactly where the red-tailed hawk lives in the woods nearby. I eat better, I sleep better, I get more exercise. I used to work out in a gym; the state forest is my gym now. If I'm working too hard, the outdoors calls to me. Thank goodness for the Land Bank, one of the most brilliant moves a legislative body can make to preserve a place," she adds.

I ask Debbie if there's anything about the Vineyard that she doesn't love.

"Yes," she quickly admits, "it can be a real hassle to orchestrate our comings and goings on and off the island. Without online shopping and Fed Ex and UPS and DHL we couldn't live here. We couldn't run our business. And it's expensive. It's easy to find a $500 sweater, but it's hard to find $5 underwear. Yet, she is quick to add, "It's worth the struggle. It really is."

⌘

Debbie

Debra Phillips has been an executive and life coach since 1995. She brings to the island twenty years of professional experience as a newspaper reporter, as the press secretary to Ohio Governor Richard Celeste, and as president of U.S. Health Productions Company. Debbie earned a master's degree in public administration at the Kennedy School of Government. She is the founder of Women on Fire Events and author of the book <u>Women on Fire: Twenty Inspiring Women Share Their Life Secrets (and Save Ten Years of Struggle)</u>. A native of Ohio, Debbie has lived year round in West Tisbury since 2001 with her husband Rob Berkeley and their cat Wilbur.

Dave

Postmaster

"You're 1346!" Dave said, pointing his finger and laughing.

Amazing, I thought. This man had worked at the West Tisbury Post Office for six years but left the island three years ago. How did he remember my post office box number?

"Hey, that's what I do," he said, in answer to my look of surprise.

Dave, a Swansea native, worked in the Fall River Post Office until twelve years ago. His brother was a state trooper doing summer service on Martha's Vineyard.

"The Vineyard may not be the place you spend the rest of your life," his brother told Dave, "but it's a heck of a place to watch the world go by. Come on over."

Dave accepted the invitation and spent his first night on Martha's Vineyard in the State Police barracks. He returned for the chili festival and then again and again to join the friends he made easily. It was no surprise that he answered an ad to work in the Vineyard Haven Post Office. He was offered the job and slated to begin work in January 1998.

"A friend and I came with bikes to find a place to live," Dave says. "But no luck. We stopped in Papa's Pizza (now Pomodoro's) and met Joanne Philbrook working there. She rented me a room in her home in Oak Bluffs for $100 a week."

"That's the way it always is on the Vineyard," Dave says. "You run into the right people at the right time. Then I did the Vineyard shuffle, moving from place to place. I stayed for a year and a half, then, thinking I'd find a better life, I left for New

Hampshire, but I missed the Vineyard. I came back to visit friends. Within two hours I had two job offers—one at the West Tisbury Post Office and one at the Hot Tin Roof. Something was telling me I belonged on the Vineyard."

For the next six years Dave, known at the post office as "Big Dave," worked happily. "You wouldn't believe all the great people I met," he says. "Once I was at a friend's dinner party when Peter Farrelly, the big Hollywood producer. We knew each other because he picked up his mail at the post office. He was doing a movie about the Red Sox. 'Fever Pitch,' it was called."

"Want to be in the movies, Dave?" Farrelly asked.

"Do I what?"

"Want to be in a movie?"

"Of course!"

So Dave turned out to be an "extra" in a Fenway Park crowd. He tells me to look for him at the start of the movie if I ever get to see it.

"It doesn't end there," he continues. "Peter invited me to a cookout at his home at Upper Makonikey on the Sound." Dave stops en route to the cookout to buy a six-pack of beer. When he arrives at Farrelly's home, he finds caterers and a full spread. "Jim Belushi and his wife and kids showed up while I was eating my burger. A bunch of guys from the Bruins were there. Cam Neely was there. In walked Kate and Livingston Taylor and Harold Ramis, who wrote *Ghostbusters, Animal House, Analyze This, Stripes*. The sun was going down with the Elizabeth Islands in the background. This could never happen to a regular guy like me anywhere else!

"I moved twelve times," Dave tells me. "But for five years I stayed with my friend Joe in a bachelor pad in Vineyard Haven. It was a mishmash. Every piece of furniture was third—or fourth-hand. My brother's girlfriend came to the house and said, 'This place looks like a Cardy's commercial—the *before!*' But we had fun there. We had little except a satellite package and a huge TV to watch sports. We never locked the door. We didn't even have a key. Once, when we let a friend crash there, he locked the door before he left. We had to climb in through the window when we returned!"

Dave left the Vineyard again in 2004. "I was getting the itch to go somewhere else for awhile. But by then the Vineyard had morphed into something important. I found that when people asked me where home was, I said Martha's Vineyard, not Swansea. When I learned that the postmaster job in Chilmark was open, I couldn't resist. I applied and was hired on December 24, 2005.

"Besides, I had met the woman of my dreams in Vineyard Haven. I'd be marrying her in March 2007. As a wedding gift to each other, we went to the Granary Gallery and bought a Scott Terry painting called 'The Party Never Ends'—very red and orange and glowing just like the light on the Vineyard."

"I want to be able to make enough money to afford to live here," Dave explains, "but I'm not sure I can. My wife and I talk about the $50 half-bag we get when we go to the grocery store. Off-island we can get twice as much for the money. It costs me $75 to fill my gas tank. When I go to Swansea to visit my moth-er, it costs me $200 by the time I pay for the ferry and gas, and I sometimes I have to take a day off from work besides. And the ferry is another thing. You feel like a teenager with a curfew—if you don't make the 8:30 boat in the wintertime, you stay on the mainland till morning. Or, if you haven't made a reservation, you get up at 4:30 because the only spaces are on the 6 a.m. boat. Last winter it cost us $3,000 to buy natural gas to heat our rental house. Middle class people are really squeezed here. I have a good secure job and still take a second job in the summertime just to make ends meet. Ordinary people like plumbers and carpenters and electricians struggle to stay on the island. My wife and I want

Dave monitoring a rural postal route

to build a good life together. We want to have a family. We're not sure we can do that here, as much as the Vineyard feels like home."

Dave

Dave Medeiros, *known as "Big Dave" when he worked at the West Tisbury Post Office, is currently the postmaster in Chilmark. He has tried to leave the Vineyard, but the island repeatedly draws him "back home." He likes simple pleasures, friendly people, and an occasional opportunity to play a small part in a movie. Dave lives in West Tisbury with his wife. He reports that she has made certain that all their furniture matches.*

Terry

Conservationist

"It is said that I was conceived on the island," remarked Terry. "My birthday is in March, so it could be true. My family spent the month of July each year, from the 1940s to 1986, in my parents' East Chop cottage. I never made a decision to settle on Martha's Vineyard. I always knew I would. There was nothing to decide.

"The Julys of my youth were a medley of activity," Terry tells me. "The East Chop Beach Club down the hill from our cottage was an oasis from the rest of the island. We loved swim lessons and shuffleboard and ping-pong and running to the tennis courts only a few blocks away. In the evenings I'd lie on my bed, often with a friend who spent the night, and, with windows wide open and breezes blowing, we'd talk and listen to the ferry whistle as we fell asleep.

"Every girl has a 'best friend' and mine, Beverly, lived right next door," Terry remembers. "We were inseparable during those elementary school years and right on through high school, and our friendship continues today. Beverly's mother didn't cook, and I felt very special when her family invited me out to dinner with them. Our families gathered together with about a dozen other summer families to enjoy the Fourth of July fireworks in Edgartown, but Beverly and I had our private escapades too. We loved the penny candy store next to the merry-go-round—just couldn't decide which to buy. Wax lips? Turkish taffy? Pez? Necco wafers? Braided strings of licorice? Wax bottles filled with red and green and yellow and orange elixir or sugar dots that peeled off a strip of paper? We spent hours there honing our decision-making skills. When we weren't there, we were in Hilliard's chocolate store deciding between chocolate turtles and peanut butter fudge. Sometimes we'd go with my grandmother up-island on State Road to Farmer Greene's place where we bought all our vegetables. On other days we'd fish from the jetty in Oak Bluffs with a piece of string and a bit of bacon as our bait."

Terry's childhood memories fuel her passion to conserve the resources of this island. "I remember when the distance between the road and the East Chop cliffs was ten feet," she says. "Now there are places with only one to two feet of edge between the land and the ocean." She remembers, too, the outings to up-island sites that are private today. "We'd love to be taken to 'the shacks'—open beach cottages in Chilmark—where we'd change our clothes to swim. We'd picnic at South Beach. My sister and I would pile into my father's jeep and bounce through the woods and dirt roads of East Chop and later on the rough terrain around Eel Pond in Edgartown on property now marked 'private.' That's why I especially love to go on the Conservation Society and Land Bank and Trustees of Reservation walks on Sundays in the off-season—they give us access to places that were open to all once upon a time."

I ask Terry if she remembers when the island changed, and she tells me a story. "During my college years, a lot of hippies came to the island," she said. Summer cottages, boarded and abandoned, were a lure. She remembers the call from her mother telling her about the fire in their summer cottage. A fisherman on the Sound saw the flames. It was too late. The cottage burned to the ground. The perpetrators were never caught, but it was clear that they had tried to keep warm by building a fire and then escaped when the fire grew out of control. "This event was a watershed for me," she confesses. "It seemed that, after that era, the island became less open, more privatized, more proprietary."

Terry tells me that the good side of the early hippie years was the coffee house on Circuit Avenue where she heard Tom Rush and other blues and folk singers of the Sixties. "It was a very laidback time. We brought our army blankets to Vineyard Haven to watch The Yale Drama Society perform Shakespeare in the Park at Tashmoo. Each town had a baseball team—ours was the Brewers. We hooted and whistled and cheered for our town's team on Soldier's Field at the end of Circuit Avenue."

"The island was changing, but the people were the same," Terry says. "Next to the beautiful ocean vistas, that was the lure of the place. All winter long my family anticipated the joy of returning the next summer to a place where friends and community activities were so easy to enjoy. That became my goal, too.

"Though I was successful and happy with my job in Washington, D.C., a divorce convinced me that I needed to make a change in my life. I bought my own place in East Chop. What a difference it was from the 1880s row house I renovated in D.C! I had never seen the backside of Crystal Lake until a realtor brought me to a small year-round cottage, formerly a one-room cabin, built in 1925. It had a fireplace and a closet-sized bathroom uncovered during subsequent renovation. A view of the Sound! This is it! I bought it, knowing that I would have to rent it every summer for ten years to be able to afford it, but that was a small sacrifice to make to be able to live on the Vineyard. The good fortune of finding and buying that East Chop cottage continued when I married my husband John. He was as enamored of the Vineyard as I was. In August of 2003, we decided to put our home in D.C. up for sale. By September 2 it sold. By September 30, we became full-time residents of the Vineyard, hopefully forever. We live in a wet area at the edge of a pond. My astilbe likes wet feet and grows to four feet around. In the spring we have a carpet of daffodils followed by native purple iris. The rhododendron flourish. We do too."

Terry buried in rhododendron

"You were a summer resident for so many years. Was there any tension between the islanders and the summer folk?" I ask. Terry is quick to respond, "The summer people care very much about the community, and many, as I did, choose to come here to spend the rest of their lives. I don't feel like a wash-ashore. I feel an important part of this community. 'Wash-ashore' is a misnomer. There's a lot of talent and energy in people who choose to live here and contribute to island life, even though they weren't born here. My career took me to Washington, D.C," Terry says. "I served in executive and managerial jobs. Now I transfer my skills to help with community development and water quality on Martha's Vineyard. I'm proud to be able to contribute the skill set I developed throughout my career to this wonderful island. I don't feel like an outsider when I serve on a committee helping to develop the Island Plan. My ideas are well received. I feel I can contribute."

Terry confesses that she worries a lot about our water quality and misuse of our natural resources. "Waste control, water, transportation, and building control are essential to keep the island rural and charming and open for the future. The natural resources are the best thing about the island. Life on the Vineyard has introduced me to amazing people. Among them are some who fish, some who paint, and some who can name every one of the island's birds. They have taught me to appreciate the ocean, the ponds, and open space that make the Vineyard such a cherished way of life."

༄

Terry

Terry Appenzellar is a graduate of Connecticut College but is proudest of earning her MBA from Wharton Business School at the University of Pennsylvania after the age of forty. During her business career in Washington, D.C., she worked on global implementations of enterprise systems and diverse projects ranging from managing air traffic control software to evaluating U.S. immigration systems. She currently serves on the boards of the Vineyard Conservation Society and the Friends of Sengekontacket. She is a member of the Oak Bluffs Community Development Council, and she has served as treasurer of the Dukes County Health Council. Terry sings in the Island Community Chorus and is a member of the Garden Club. She and her husband John live in the East Chop section of Oak Bluffs.

Kim

Parent and Advocate

Eager feet kicked up dust from the dry summer fields adjoining the West Tisbury Agricultural Hall in August 2007. My husband Dan and I walked the pathways of the annual Agricultural Fair of Dukes County. Farmers, crafts persons, artists, and a medley of livestock lovers traipsed around the fair grounds to the accompaniment of carnival music and the squeals of excited children riding the Ferris wheel into the sky.

I wasn't thinking of finding *Island Home* interviewees that day as I, too, explored the Ag Fair, at least not until I came upon the Human Race Machine a few steps away from the Homemade Strawberry Shortcake booth and across from the Firemen's Famous Hamburger stand.

My old friend Bob, assistant principal of the West Tisbury School, beckoned me enthusiastically. "You've got to see this, Elaine," he said. Kim, who was overseeing the machine, greeted me warmly. She had been an active parent when I was principal of the West Tisbury School a few years earlier. Today, though, her focus was on diversity.

"Did you ever wonder what you'd look like if you were African-American?" she asked me. "Or Asian, or Indian, or Middle Eastern?"

"Not really," I replied honestly.

She sat me in the Human Race Machine, and, within ten minutes, her question was answered. The machine photographed me, and the software, programmed to the subtle nuances of ethnic identity features, converted my Caucasian face into an African-American one, then an Asian face, an Indian face, a Hispanic face, and a Middle Eastern face.

"I love me as an Indian," I exclaimed. Dan, whose turn on the machine followed mine, preferred himself as an African-American.

This chance encounter at the Ag Fair gave us not only new faces but deeper awareness of how unique our own faces would look if we were born into a different race.

"Where did you get this machine?" I asked Bob.

"Kim and her friend Monica found it and worked hard to bring it to the island," he replies.

"Were you born here?" I asked Kim.

"No," she replied, "but I've lived here for seventeen years. This is my home."

"Let's talk," I invited her.

Kim was born and raised in the shore town of Pawcatuck, near Mystic, Connecticut. She tells me that she took the sea for granted. She also took for granted the ability to walk safely on the streets at night. Lured by the glitz of Los Angeles, the people, and the frenetic activity, she found work in the international mortgage field on Wilshire Boulevard. "My commute was brutal," she tells me. "I moved to Brentwood, but it took three more years to realize that my roots were in New England. I was a New England gal—too many free spirits for me on the California scene," she confesses.

"I was very analytical in my thinking. I'll try Boston, I thought. It's still a city and an exciting place, but it's smaller than Los Angeles. Boston might work. And it did, until I met the Vineyard." Kim first came to Martha's Vineyard as a tourist to Oak Bluffs. "Unlike most folks, I first came in the wintertime," she tells me. "It was 1986—I was approaching the magic age of thirty."

"I had to give up a new car to settle on the Vineyard," Kim admits. "I was a credit analyst in Boston, and I was saving money for a fancy car. One day I realized that buying that car would bind me to the Boston job and to car payments in addition. It's time to re-think this, I said to myself."

Kim searching titles at the County Courthouse in Edgartown

In 1990 she took the car savings, rented a place in Vineyard Haven, and wrote poetry on the beach for six months. "Halfway through that time, I knew I'd stay," she says. "My values had changed. Cities were no longer alluring. I had seen the maelstrom that materialism could create. I wanted a simpler, safer life."

Kim created that life, finding jobs in the banking and mortgage industry, meeting and marrying her husband David, moving from Vineyard Haven to Edgartown to West Tisbury, and giving birth to her son Jacob in 1994. She never regretted her decision to settle on Martha's Vineyard, but she did discover a way in which she could serve the community.

"The towns are Balkanized," she tells me. "Groups stay together. Few African-Americans live in West Tisbury, for example. Lots more live in Oak Bluffs. My boy was happy at the West Tisbury School. He made great friends. But he was different. Once, when he was only seven, he told a classmate that he thought a certain little girl was cute. The classmate told him that he couldn't like the little girl because he was black and she was white. I don't blame the classmate. Racism is everywhere. Similar incidents occurred as Jacob grew older. I wanted my son to understand and appreciate that difference in an accepting and loving way. I found other parents and even some educators who felt the same. We started a diversity council. The Human Race Machine was our first big project."

The Human Race Machine, a diversity-training tool used by colleges, was available for lease at a cost of $4,500. Kim and her committee were convinced that they could raise the funds, and they did. Generous sponsors such as the Dukes County Bar Association, the Martha's Vineyard Cooperative Bank, and the Hebrew Center responded to their appeal. Kim and her group held a barbecue fundraiser to raise the rest of the money.

Restaurants such as the Beach Plum Inn, Lattanzi's, David Ryan's, the Wharf, and Among the Flowers donated creative box lunches that were auctioned off at Kim's home along with other items. David, Kim's husband, was the auctioneer. "We did it," she says proudly, "We raised more than $4,500."

"What's next?" I ask Kim.

"A sign language initiative," she tells me. "The diversity council feels the need to increase awareness of the needs of the deaf. After all, from the Nineteenth to the mid-Twentieth Century, we had generations of a deaf community in Chilmark. At one time signing was viewed as a second language for islanders. With a large deaf population, it was a necessary way to communicate. Today most islanders don't know sign language."

I realize that Kim is contributing her sensitivity and her desire for equity to the culture of the Vineyard community. "What is the community doing for you?" I ask.

"I feel safe here," she replies. "I feel safe and comfortable in body and mind, in my views and in doing whatever is necessary to support my ideals.

"I'll never forget a morning when I lived in Edgartown, and I exercised by riding my bike at dawn. While cycling on the bike trails near the Edgartown-West Tisbury Road, I happened upon the most beautiful buck—a monster. It was huge, and its massive horns were silhouetted against the mist rising off the State Forest behind it. The buck stood, looking at me, for several minutes, then turned his head, and walked back into the State Forest. That animal felt comfortable and secure enough to stand in the middle of the road and not be threatened by a person. I was in awe. The buck is the metaphor for what I feel here—secure enough to stand in the open without running, fearless, at home."

ᏩᎳᎠᏇ

Kim

Kim Lawrence grew up in the seaport town of Pawcatuck in Connecticut. *She worked at Traveler's Insurance Company in Hartford, then she became a lending officer at banks in California and Massachusetts. Today she owns her own title research company and often may be found at the Registry of Deeds in the courthouse in Edgartown. She is also a partner in a home heating and air conditioning company. Kim is an active parent at the West Tisbury School. She lives in West Tisbury with her husband David and their son Jacob.*

Jim

Selectman and Charter School Board Member

Jim first arrived in Gay Head thirty-three years ago. Invited to share a friend's week of summer rental, he and his family traveled from New Jersey to Woods Hole, drove their car onto the ferry, and wound their way for twenty miles southward through Tisbury and West Tisbury and Chilmark, passing Squibnocket and Stonewall Ponds and south shore ocean vistas, en route to the Gay Head Cliffs, one of the highest points on the island. Their friend's rental property was located nearby on sparsely populated Moshup Trail.

His children, five-year-old Julie and two-year-old Peter, had never seen such a place, nor had their parents. "It was pristine and unspoiled," Jim tells me. "We loved it right away—Philbin Beach, the Cliffs, Menemsha, all of it. I was struck by the rural character of Gay Head, the quaintness and marvelous fishing off the jetty in Menemsha. We spent only a week, but I knew we'd return.

"Before we left Gay Head, we found a tiny rental cottage on Dogfish Bar. It was like a wooden tent. We returned to that little place for a week of vacation every year, counting the months 'til August in the midst of the New Jersey winters. It was years before we could come for two weeks. Finally, in the late Eighties, we were able to begin renting for the entire month of August."

Jim and his family thought that their simple yet idyllic vacations would last forever, but, in 1991, their landlord announced that the Dogfish Bar cottage would be used by his grown children. "It was January, in the midst of winter, when we found out," Jim tells me. "Kathy and I got into our car, drove from New

Jersey, and met with our Realtor. We had already spent some time looking at houses. Show us some lots,' we told him. 'We want to be near Moshup Trail.'"

The Realtor, David Flanders, had a three-acre lot on Briar Path—"a bit overgrown, but it may even have a bit of a water view," he said.

"Let's take a look," Jim replied. He explained that he and his wife Kathy had jobs in New Jersey and could only stay on the island for a day or two. "The fog had rolled in from the south shore and was thickening fast as we turned off South Road and took a left onto the half-mile-long dirt road called Briar Path. The lot was located on the left side of the road and hinted at a water view, but it was impossible to tell. Kathy even climbed a tree to try to see the ocean," Jim laughed, "but no luck. Still, we could afford the lot, made an offer, and it was accepted."

"Now we need a contractor," Jim told David.

"Try Emmet Carroll from Chilmark. You'll find him at the gas station in Menemsha."

"Emmet was great," Jim said. "He listened to us, took us to see a model of an Acorn home that he had constructed and helped us to decide how we'd change the design to suit our taste. We hired him and, by August, our Briar Path house was complete. And it did have a water view of 180 degrees overlooking No Man's Land! We had to rent it for the entire month of July so that we could afford to come in August. We were lucky and had the same renters for the next fifteen years until we retired and moved here full-time."

When I asked Jim whether the Vineyard had changed him in any way, he at first replied, "No, I'm the same man I was in New Jersey. I served on a school board there; I serve on the Charter School board here. I taught reading there; I tutor reading here. I was a volunteer in civic activities there; I served on the Aquinnah finance committee and later as a selectman here. No, I don't think the Vineyard changed me.

Jim en route to a meeting of the Aquinnah Selectmen

"But there is one big difference in the way people interact here as compared to my old New Jersey life," Jim conceded. "Here's a story that shows what I'm trying to say.

"It was 2003. A very contentious subject was debated in Aquinnah, with impassioned letters on both sides of the issue published in the local newspapers. It was the night the issue was to be decided by a vote of the selectmen. The hall was packed with vociferous people, some with furrowed faces, some angry, some rude, but all cared passionately about the result of the vote that had the potential to change the character of the town for years to come. It was a lose-lose situation for me. When I said, 'No,' and the issue was settled, at least temporarily, an outcry occurred. Some furrowed faces relaxed, some smiled, but many burned with rage. I voted my conscience, but I knew that, when you're a selectman, your popularity changes from one motion to another. My vote angered many people that night. I listened to the impassioned voices as they exited the hall and faded into the cold night. I was one of the last to leave. A woman who had argued bitterly against my position left the hall in front of me. She turned around when she reached the steps to the outdoors and warned, 'Careful, Jim, it's icy outside.'

"That bit of kindness speaks to the spirit of the island and especially to Aquinnah," Jim says.

I ask him to tell me more about the community he experiences in Aquinnah, twenty miles from the Steamship Authority ferry terminal and one of the most remote parts of the island.

"We are dependent upon one another," he begins. "One of the reasons that the culture of Aquinnah is so unique is that the Wampanoag tribe lives there. The tribe adds amazing cultural diversity to our town. The Wampanoag culture, heritage, and history all play out in their rituals and in their tribal government. The music, the rhythm, the dances, and the native dress of their pow-wows, outdoors on the circle near the Cliffs, draw visitors from all over the island." Jim explains that when the tribal government and the town government come to an agreement, they draw up a treaty because, "even though we're all part of the same town, the federal government has declared Wampanoag land as a territory unto itself.

"The tribe takes care of its members," Jim says, "but I worry about others, especially the young families who want to live here but who find the island inordinately expensive. I feel sorry for them. The school-age population on the island is declining because young families just can't afford to live here. Those of us who work in town government do our best to understand the economic realities of life in one of the least populated regions of the island, and we work to be fair, but, unless affordable housing initiatives save us, we're pricing ourselves right out of the middle class market.

"When I recall that first drive from cosmopolitan New Jersey to the Vineyard of the 1970s, I realize all the immeasurable gifts that this island has given to my family. My adult children and their families still return every year to enjoy this place. Each night when I walk outside onto my deck, with the moon as the only ambient light, and I hear the hoofs of the deer on the dry leaves in our yard and the roar of the ocean in the distance, I'm thankful that this place is my home."

☙

Jim

Jim Newman was born in Newark, raised in South Orange, and lived for thirty years in Berkeley Heights, New Jersey. After he returned from service in the Peace Corps in Liberia during the 1960s, he attended Fordham University to do masters and doctoral work in urban education. He serves as a selectman for the town of Aquinnah and on the board of directors of the Martha's Vineyard Charter School. Jim and Kathy, his wife of forty years, live in Aquinnah.

Part III
Why Do They Stay?

Traveling from the Past Into the Future

It is August. The ferry *Island Home* is about to leave its berth in the Vineyard Haven slip. Boxes and baggage on its overflowing luggage cart poke through the drape that is closed now as the cart is driven onto the boat. Just before the huge door lowers, securing the cars and trucks and merry-go-round and Ferris wheel parts from the recent county fair, a recorded message sounds: "Do not leave your luggage unattended. All packages are subject to inspection."

Not "subject to inspection" are the wash-ashores who stay on Martha's Vineyard, though some who were born here or who have lived here a long time tell me that it's the wash-ashores who created all the problems of today.

"What was wrong with the way we did things before? We understood each other. We were happy without all the change that came with the wash-ashores. I'm not interested in what you people did in New Jersey or New York or Connecticut or anywhere else," one longtime resident said to me recently.

But I don't see growth and change as a negative. I believe that the newcomers add to the diversity already here. They've integrated our communities of Mayhews and Alleys and Nortons and Vanderhoops and deepened the texture of this place. They're also concerned about runaway development, about depletion of natural resources, about good governance, schools, and libraries. After a while, you can't tell the difference between a native and a wash-ashore.

Why do these wash-ashores, those whom I interviewed, stay on Martha's Vineyard? Most are not rich, at least not financially. Many speak about the financial hardships of maintaining a life on the Vineyard. "Why must I pay $3.29 for a dozen eggs that I can buy for $1.89 on the mainland?" one asks me. Many had successful lives elsewhere—as teachers or professors or ministers, as laborers or fishermen, as corporate leaders or entrepreneurs. Embedded in some of their stories is a hint of the anxieties that propelled them to change their lives, the struggle to overcome obstacles, and the commitment that each has made to this island and its communities. For most, the move to the island was not perfect, nor has the struggle to live comfortably been easy. Still, there was an upbeat tone to most of the interviews because, simply, despite the drawbacks of island living, these islanders are delighted to have settled on Martha's Vineyard.

Reflecting on the completed interviews made me realize that the interview stories parallel an important sociological happening on this island. The life of families has changed dramatically since some sixty- and seventy- and eighty-year-olds summered here as children. Few families "summer" any more. Gone are the days when housewife mothers packed their children for a full summer on the Vineyard and corporate fathers visited on weekends and during vacation time. Today we have more dual working parents and fewer summer properties owned by young families. Visits to grandparents still happen, but fewer young families spend the entire summer on this island.

Not only have the lifestyles of families changed during the past forty years, but the Vineyard has become grayer too. Many young families, service workers, and middle class people struggle with the financial hardships of living here, and some have simply given up and moved off-island. Affordable housing initiatives will help, but I suspect that the need will be far greater than the demand. By 2018, we expect a twenty per cent decline in school age children. As a result, the median age of those whom I interviewed, those who have made a lifetime commitment to remain here, is fifty, not thirty.

The Trustees of Reservations maintain sylvan paths at Long Point

Before we began our interview session, I asked each intervie-
wee to brainstorm words that describe Martha's Vineyard.
Brainstorming involves free association, the jotting down of
descriptive words and phrases without judgment. Each wrote as
many words as they could muster in a timed five-minute period.
In the end, I compared their responses. Four mentioned the light
of this island. "The light is different here," they said later in their
interviews. "I can't describe it. It's clearer and brighter and beautiful and the tease of artists and photographers who try to cap-
ture it." As each of the fourteen brainstormed, adjectives such as
"peaceful, serene, pastoral, and beautiful" were used repeatedly
to describe the setting. "Natural, accepting, invigorating, and
friendly" described the people.

During the interviews, the themes of extended family and community echoed again and again. In some cases, people could never have remained on the island without the vigilance and love of newfound neighbors, friends, and protectors. Mary's story is emblematic of that. The richness of the island's history shines through the stories of Allan, Peter, and Terry. The freedom of people to be themselves reverberates from Janet and Alison. Vicky and Debbie describe the gentle features of the island and the solace in even the rain and fog. Suzan celebrates the birds and marshlands and estuaries. Elaine is energized by the culture and all the ways to "give back." Jim notes the interdependence of those who live on Martha's Vineyard. Isaque tells of the home he was able to buy after seventeen years of struggle. Dave worries that he may never be able to afford his own home, yet, each time he leaves the island, it begs him to return. Many describe the island's *magnetism,* its inexplicable draw. Nearly everyone speaks of the pleasure of living on an island where doors are never locked and where people can walk the byways and the beaches at any hour of the day or night.

Each of the people who granted me an interview adds an important dimension to the hardy stock of deep-rooted and caring natives who shepherded this island for generations. They are not simply consumers of the island's magical qualities; they are active participants in its daily life, and they contribute to its culture. Many work alongside the Vineyard-born to keep the island healthy and to plan wisely for its future. Some promote a deeper understanding of the arts and music. Others teach us to respect the delicate balance of the physical features that surround us. Many belong to local philanthropic organizations, and some lead our volunteer boards. Some are models of a relentless work ethic. Others are advocates for equity. Some teach us to see our surroundings in a new way. One or two remind us to laugh at our foibles, to appreciate our blessings, and to trust the resilience of human nature.

These "newcomers" are only a small portion of the eighteen thousand dynamic people who make their homes here year-round. Whether they came to the Vineyard to pursue a job or to create a business, to simplify their lives or to find solace, to search for youthful memories or to retire into old age, each has become an important thread in the fabric of this island. The synergy of the old and the new, native and newcomer, gives us hope that together we can move wisely into the future.

The ferry *Island Home* departs now, winding its way out of the harbor, through the Sound, past the Elizabeth Islands and on to the familiar port of Woods Hole where it empties itself of the transient tourists who may or may not return. En route from Woods Hole to Vineyard Haven is the vintage ship *Martha's Vineyard*. On the horizon to the northwest is the New Bedford fast ferry, emblematic of ongoing change. The tourist season is nearly over. By October Martha's Vineyard will belong once again to all those who call it their island home.

ᏔᏍᎤ

Driftwood and footprints at summer's end

Printed in the United States
203441BV00001B/1-105/P